Group Work:
An international conversation
highlighting diversity in practice

Proceedings of the XXXIV International Symposium
on Social Work with Groups
Long Island, New York, USA, June 14-17, 2012

Group Work:

An international conversation
highlighting diversity in practice

Edited by

**Gregory J. Tully, Jean Bacon,
Georgianna Dolan-Reilly, & Alexandra Lo Re**

w&b

MMXIII

© Whiting & Birch Ltd 2013
Published by Whiting & Birch Ltd,
Forest Hill, London SE23 3HZ

ISBN 9781861771346

Printed in England and the United States by Lightning Source

CONTENTS

About the Editors

Greg Tully, PhD, is an Associate Professor at West Chester University in West Chester, Pennsylvania. His academic experience includes twelve years at Iona College, where he served as Chair of the Social Work Department, and five years as Associate Professor at Barry University. Greg has also taught individual clinical practice and group work on the faculties of New York University and Hunter College School of Social Work. His social work practice areas include: work with victims of trauma, including spouse abuse, rape, and child sexual abuse; HIV/AIDS; organizational leadership coaching; and juvenile probation. Dr. Tully has presented plenary, invitational, and workshop presentations internationally on a variety of subjects. His writing has been published in the Encyclopedia of Social Work with Groups, the Journal of Teaching in Social Work, and the Journal of Baccalaureate Social Work. He is President of the International Association for Social Work with Groups.

Jean Bacon, Ph.D., is currently the Executive Director at Butterfly, a community mental health agency. She served on the faculty at Stony Brook University's School of Social Welfare for fifteen years. She has experience teaching practice, group work, and treatment of children and adolescents. Dr. Bacon's research areas include bereavement, grief reactions, cultural diversity, and HIV/AIDS. She has practiced for over 20 years utilizing individual, family, and group treatment modalities. Her ongoing training experience includes educating child welfare workers about: leadership development, stress reduction, and understanding and treating child abuse and maltreatment. She has presented both nationally and internationally on subjects related to building community, treatment issues, diversity, and group work. She has published in a number of journals and continues to support social work education and group work. Dr. Bacon co-chaired the 2012 IASWG Symposium in Long Island, NY. and serves as a committee member of the IASWG Recruitment Retention Project.

Georgianna Dolan-Reilly, LMSW, is Chief Editor, Board Member, and a Staff Writer at Social Justice Solutions. Georgianna received her master's in Social Welfare from Stony Brook University in 2012. As a student, she interned as a School Social Worker and School Health Policy Specialist. Georgianna has research experience in the areas of Autism Spectrum Disorders, cognition and perception, sexuality, healthy lifestyles, quality of life, and medical research. As a social worker, she is particularly interested in group and community work as it relates to preventative and public health. In addition, she is interested in restrictive diet and food allergen management from a psychosocial perspective, political social work and policy, work with youth, and social work education and research. For IASWG, Georgianna served as Student Volunteer Coordinator for the 2012 IASWG Long Island Symposium, and is currently serving as a committee member for the IASWG Recruitment Retention Project and the IASWG Symposium Planning Committee.

Alexandra Lo Re, LMSW, received her master's degree in social work from Adelphi University in May, 2012. Before entering Adelphi, Alexandra worked as an assistant editor for a curriculum-based publishing company in Manhattan. As a student in her social work graduate program, she interned at an early-elementary school and a pediatric psychiatric facility. In both settings, Alexandra centered her study on the use of group work as an effective intervention for traumatized children and families. She also worked as a research assistant and presented at both the 2011 and 2012 IASWG symposia. Additionally, Alexandra was on the Planning Committee for the 2012 IASWG Long Island Symposium, and served as the Student Volunteer Coordinator. Currently, Alexandra assists patients in need of stabilization, counseling, and community outreach as a social worker in an adult Comprehensive Psychiatric Emergency Program in a New York City hospital.

The Contributors

Eleanor Avinor, PhD, MSc in Psychotherapy, MA, is a psychotherapist at Bnei Zion Hospital, and past professor at the University of Haifa, Haifa, Israel. She is also the creator of KEG (Keys to Emotional Growth) cards, a recently developed therapeutic tool. Email: eleanav@research. haifa.ac.il

Robert Basso, RSW, is a faculty member in the Social Work Department at Wilfrid Laurier University, Waterloo, Ontario, Canada. Dr. Basso has practiced group work in several practice arenas: children's groups, addictions, intimate violence, and sexually assaulted males. He has taught group work for twenty five years at the MSW level. Email: rbasso@wlu.ca

Kathryn K. Berg, LSW, MA (in Women's Studies and Gender Studies), is a recent graduate of Loyola University in Chicago. She is currently employed as a Community Support Specialist at Thresholds, and is working toward clinical licensure while preparing to pursue a doctorate in social work. Research and scholarship interests include: group work, intersectionality theory, White identity development, issues of gender violence, and spirituality in social work. Email: berg.kathrynk@gmail. com

Ginette Berteau, is a social worker and professor at the School of Social Work at the University of Quebec, Montreal (UQAM, Canada) where she has worked for 13 years. She has always been a passionate believer in social group work, and this enthusiasm has led her to do group work, train and supervise group work social workers and students, earn a PhD in the skills specific to group work, and to publish a book on the subject. Email: berteau.ginette@uqam.ca

Willa J. Casstevens, PhD, MSW, LCSW, is an Associate Professor for the Department of Social Work at North Carolina State University, Raleigh, North Carolina, USA, where she also oversees the North

Carolina State University's Suicide Prevention Program. She has experience in the field of mental health prevention, assessment, and intervention. Email: wjcasste@ncsu.edu

Leslie Cloninger, MSW, is a recent graduate from North Carolina State University, and is now a Social Worker in Chapel Hill, North Carolina, USA. Email: lesliecloninger@gmail.com

Colleen Egan-Mascolo, LCSW, is a social worker and a group co-facilitator at NSLIJ Zucker Hillside Hospital's Mineola Community Treatment Center, Mineola, NY, USA. She works with adolescents and adults struggling with substance abuse. Email: cegan@nshs.edu

Eva Feindler, Ph.D., is the Director of the Clinical Psychology Doctoral Program, and professor of psychology, at Long Island University, Brookville, NY. Eva was instrumental in the development of anger management programs for teens and their families across the United States and Europe, and is a founding member of the International Center for Aggression Replacement Training based in Sweden. Email: Eva.Feindler@liu.edu

Loretta Hartley-Bangs, LCSW, is the current Program Director of the Mineola Community Treatment Center, NSLIJ Zucker Hillside Hospital, Mineola, NY, USA. She is also an adjunct professor in the Social Work Departments at both Molloy College and Long Island University-CW Post. She has a 28 year history of working in substance abuse and mental health. Email: lbangs@optonline.net

Judith A. B. Lee, RCWP, DSW, MSW, DMin, is Professor Emeritus of the University of Connecticut School of Social Work, and Priest and Co-Pastor at the Good Shepherd Inclusive Catholic Community, Fort Myers, Florida, USA. Judy is past President of IASWG, serving from 1985-1991, and has an extensive background as social work educator and group work leader. Email: judyabl@embarqmail.com

P. Matthew Lozano is currently an MSW student at Loyola University in Chicago, Chicago, IL, USA. Email: matthew.lozano@gmail.com

Masoomeh Maarefvand, PhD, is a social worker, located at the University of Social Welfare and Rehabilitation Sciences, Social Work Department, Tehran, Iran. Email: arammaref@gmail.com

Marisa D. Mahler, Psy.D., is a Clinical Psychologist specializing in anxiety, depression, Adjustment Disorders, and relationship issues. She is located in New York, NY, USA. Email: drmarisamahler@gmail.com

Ellen Sue Mesbur, MSW, Ed.D, is a Professor in the School of Social Work at Renison University College, University of Waterloo, Canada, where she served as director for ten years. She is a distinguished teacher and group work leader, and In 2012 was recognized by CASWE for her contributions to social work education in Canada, and by IASWG for her contributions to IASWG and to social group work education as the 2012 International Honouree. Email: ellensuemesbur@sympatico.ca

William Pelech, PhD, RSW, is Associate Professor and Faculty in the department of Social Work at the University of Calgary, Alberta, Canada. Dr. Pelech has an extensive research background in interpersonal communication in treatment groups, and has published several articles relating to the practitioner's use of diversity in group work practice. Email: pelech@ucalgary.ca

Lauren A. Phillips, MSW, is a recent graduate of Loyola University in Chicago. She works for the   Lorene Replogle Counseling Center, Chicago, Illinois, USA. Email: lphillips1@luc.edu

Maryam Sadat Mirmalek Sani, MA, is located at Comprehensive Scientific and Applied University (Culture and Art), Tehran, Iran. Email: mirmalekmaryam@yahoo.com

Shirley R. Simon, ACSW, LCSW is Associate Professor for the School of Social Work at Loyola University in Chicago, Illinois, USA. She has been a social work educator for over thirty years, has published on group work education, practice and history; she has facilitated over one hundred presentations at professional conferences. Research and scholarship interests include: group work education in MSW programs, hybrid-online group work instruction, curricular strategies for connecting students and professional associations, and social work dissertations on group work. Email: ssimon@luc.edu

Jorune Vysniauskyte Rimkiene, MSW, PhD, is a lecturer of Social Work at Vytautas Magnus University, Kaunas, Lithuania. Email: j.r j.rimkiene@sgi.vdu.lt

Emily Wilk, MSW, is a recent graduate of Loyola University in Chicago. She is now Assistant Director for Adventure Recreation and Camps, University of Dayton, Dayton, Ohio, USA. Email: ewilk@luc.edu

Louise Warin is a social worker, a trainer at FOPA (open university), and an educator at HELMo ESAS (School of Social Work, University College, Liège, Belgium) for the past 13 years. She has been working with women's groups for 20 years. She shares her passion for group work by teaching future social workers. Her interest in training students to do social work with groups led her to work with the UQAM school of social work. Email: louisewarin@gmail.com

Mary Wilson, PhD, is Senior Lecturer at the School of Applied Studies, University College Cork, Ireland. Email: m.wilson@ucc.ie

Acknowledgements

Association for the Advancement of Social Work with Groups, Inc.
XXXIV Annual International Symposium
Long Island, New York, June 14-17, 2012

Symposium International Honoree
Ellen Sue Mesbur

Symposium Local Honorees:
Lois Carey
Beverly Feigelman
Samuel Goldstein
Loretta Hartley-Bangs
Andrew Malekoff
Edwin Simon
Louise Skolnik

Symposium Co-Chairs
Jean Bacon
Steve Kraft

Many thanks for the tremendous support received from Stony Brook University School of Social Welfare and Adelphi University School of Social Work. The assistance from both universities created a wonderful collaboration. Special thanks to our Adelphi University supporters: Carol, Gina, and Anthony. Each of them went beyond what was asked of them to strengthen our relationship with Adelphi.

Much appreciation for the efforts of Beverly Feigelman, Lois Carey, Nancy Burke, Sari Skolnick, Pam Brodlieb, Sam Goldstein, Loretta Hartley-Bangs, Jacqueline Lederman, Alexandra Lo Re, Georgianna Dolan-Reilly, Andrew Malekoff, Jonathan Orgel, Audrey Sena, Deirdre Weliky, Carol Cohen, Ed Simon, Karen Herring, and the entire Long Island Symposium Planning Committee. We gratefully acknowledge their hard work and support. Thanks also to the student volunteers from the various schools of social work, and the many IASWG Board members who were supportive and helpful throughout the process.

Thank you to the many authors in this volume who contributed their scholarly writing. Much appreciation for joining us on this project.

And lastly, a special thank you to David Whiting, our publisher. Without his guidance and support we could not have developed and produced this volume.

Tribute

This volume is dedicated to Katy Papell and Steve Kraft. Both Katy and Steve have provided much inspiration both personally and professionally to each of the four editors of this volume. The two have known each other since meeting at Adelphi University in 1974, and been connected ever since by their love of group work and their dedicated service to the IASWG Long Island Chapter.

Katy Papell is a group work icon, and she encourages group workers everywhere to engage in group work education, research, practice, and most especially advocacy. Katy blessed us with her presence and her wisdom at the Long Island Symposium, and she has always raised the banner for social work with groups. Katy attended the first group work symposium, June 19, 1978, in Cleveland, and she has never stopped celebrating the power of group work. She has taught many social work students and professionals the value and sustaining nature of the group process. We are all fortunate to have been touched by her magic.

Steve Kraft has always championed group work, practicing group work with young men, child welfare workers, and several other populations. He has also taught group work to social work students. Steve has served as the President of the International Association for Social Work with Groups from 2009 through 2012, volunteered as the IASWG attorney for many years to negotiate and advocate for the needs of IASWG, and Co-chaired the 2012 IASWG Long Island Symposium during a time in his life of personal challenge. He has always encouraged all of us to discuss and debate the opportunities presented by group work with diverse populations, and he continues to promote research, education and practice of the social group work method.

Both Steve and Katy were present at the 2012 Long Island Symposium Invitational session dedicated to Katy. It was at this session that Katy spoke briefly but powerfully. Emotions ran high and tears ran freely as Katy rose from her wheelchair to stand in front of her colleagues, young and old, to stress the responsibility of all group workers to continue to promote group work practice, and to call for the new generation of group workers to assume the task of maintaining group work prominence. Her words will forever remain with us:

I am indeed blessed – I have lived 95 ½ years. You are such a precious part of those years. It was 34 years ago that a surge of social work educators who believed in group life as a vital part of social work's helping role in society decided to say so, very loudly, so the profession would cease forgetting. The result was an annual group work symposium. I am not the only one here tonight who was there in Boston at the Council on Social Work Education (CSWE) meeting, March 19, 1978, and then at the first group work Symposium, June 19, 1978 in Cleveland. Yes, we social workers with groups know how to do it. I was with you in the affirming, planning, and holding of a glorious professional social work with groups meeting. And I am so lucky to be here tonight, even if in a wheelchair, to see what we have become. In your wonderful social work selves lies the responsibility for helping the grouping to keep on grouping, in and out of the profession. I must tell you that one of you, Ann Bergart, is preparing a book based on my published and unpublished writing about social work with groups. And my beloved social work daughter, Linda Papell Kwiatek, has done what would seem impossible, saving all my papers from the disorder of moving out of my home of 50 years. She has gallantly put everything in order for Ann's choosing and selecting. Yes, I am so fortunate to be here tonight, and I go away, probably never to come back again, with permanent warmth in my heart, the kind of magical feeling that we group workers know is produced by human kind finding human kind in their lives together in groups. Yes, I, Katy Papell have indeed lucked out.

Introduction

Group work:
An international conversation highlighting diversity in practice

In a time of rising uncertainty, it has never been more important to embrace our differences, to celebrate our unique abilities, and to highlight our global connections. Representing group work authors from many countries (Lithuania, Israel, Belgium, Canada, Iran, Ireland, and the United States), it is our pleasure to share with you our eleven chapters on social group work, each highlighting the diversity and global identity of social group work practice. These chapters, the result of the scholarship shared at the 34th Annual International Association for Social Work with Groups (IASWG) Symposium, represent the work of group workers across the world, and reflect the diversity found within the global community of group work practitioners.

The 34th Annual IASWG Symposium, held in 2012, in Long Island, New York, USA, was dedicated to the international passion of group work. Long Island, a historic place, served as an inspirational backdrop for many scholarly presentations. Long Island is known as a location of lovely beaches, bridges, and ocean views, and Long Island is the home of a cherished international IASWG chapter. The Long Island IASWG Symposium theme, "Passion for Group Work: An International Conversation", promoted the value of increased group work practice in global communities. The IASWG Symposium, paired with the International Interdisciplinary Conference on Clinical Supervision, also advocated for the increased sharing of knowledge among group work professionals throughout the world.

The Symposium event began with a showcase of various talents, including vocal performances of Irish songs, a poetry reading in Arabic, and group sing-a-longs of songs from a variety of countries. Jean Bacon and Steve Kraft, Co-Chairs, welcomed all of us the first night, as did the members of the Long Island Symposium Planning Committee. As the night progressed, and shyness gave way to familiarity, the Symposium attendees began experiencing the shift that occurs when a group starts to find its rhythm. Laughter and applause are universal, and through them that first night we were able to connect with each other even when language differences failed us. For as many groups discover, our supposed differences only mask the numerous commonalities we share.

There are few places that invoke the spirit of cooperative global scholarship like a university; the university campus is a natural meeting ground for individuals to discuss topics, debate theories, and challenge one another. A university teems with energy, and it often is a place where many of us first discover our passion for group work. Adelphi University, in Garden City, New York, USA, hosted the 34th Annual Symposium for the International Association for Social Work with Groups. The Adelphi University site provided the opportunity for honoring our academic origins, as well as looking toward our future possibilities as group workers in the global community.

Reflecting on the symposium weekend, it occurred to us that while we certainly fostered an international dialogue, we also managed to transcend additional boundaries. By remembering our past and paying tribute to it, we encouraged both our newest and our youngest members to embrace and celebrate our mission. Many students and recent graduates gathered with teachers and mentors to explore and discuss a variety of group work theories and concepts. We honored one of our founders, Katy Papell, and we shared our history with those attendees who may carry the IASWG message forward in the future. We recognized we have a bright future due to the strong foundation of our rich past.

This volume was challenging and rewarding to produce. As we worked on it, we were amazed at how often we experienced again the emotions shared over the Symposium weekend. The plenaries, workshops, and presentations that weekend offered wonderful opportunities for global group work sharing and learning.The approximately 150 workshops, papers, and student posters shared over the weekend represented the eclectic work of group workers from many countries. The chapters in this volume reflect the diversity found in the global group work community.

Chapter One immediately focuses the reader on the themes of group work, diversity, and the global community. William Pelech and Robert Basso share a pilot study they conducted in the Calgary & Niagara regions of Canada examining the significance of diversity in group development and the achievement of group member goals. Their chapter challenges us to acknowledge that an increasingly globalized world has increased the need for more inclusive practice approaches.

Chapters Two and Three present pilot studies that target group work with the adolescent population, and each chapter highlights the unique set of challenges and possibilities of this work. In Chapter

Two, Marissa Mahler seeks to quantify key process variables related to the implementation of Cognitive Behavioral Therapy Group skills training, particularly focusing on using this theoretical approach with aggressive adolescents. Mahler's study, conducted in the U.S., establishes a foundation for future group work with adolescents that would further identify how to maximize the gains within this type of group practice setting. In Chapter Three, Loretta Hartley-Bangs and Colleen Egan reflect on their work in the U.S. at the North Shore LIJ Mineola Community Treatment Center. Their chapter describes and addresses multiple-family group work in an adolescent chemical dependency intensive outpatient program.

In *Chapter Four*, Masoomeh Maarefvand and Maryam Sadat Mirmalek Sani examine the complex issue of sexual addiction in the Iranian culture. The chapter examines how peer group interventions conducted in Iran impacted treatment retention rates, and demonstrates why group leaders must be well-versed in the perils of co-morbid addiction.

In *Chapter Five*, we are treated to the moving and insightful words of Reverend Dr. Judith Lee. Her words in this chapter, a homage to Dr. Catherine Papell, remind us of the debt of gratitude we owe to Dr. Papell and her fellow group work icons. These historic group workers from around the world have paved the way for our surviving and thriving as group work practitioners and educators.

In *Chapter Six*, Mary Wilson brings her Irish perspective to the practice of group work. Her scholarly work, conducted in Ireland, explores the issue of gatekeeping in social work education. It explores the challenge of maintaining professional standards while still ensuring that non-traditional social work students receive a full educational experience.

In *Chapter Seven*, Kathryn Berg collaborates with her mentor Shirley Simon, presenting a pilot study they conducted in a U.S. university examining an anti-racism identity for White-European-American students. The chapter includes suggestions for broader replication and implementation.

In *Chapter Eight*, Ginette Berteau and Louise Warin present, in French, the results of their joint study conducted with students registered in social group work courses at schools of social work in Montreal, Quebec, Canada and Liège, Belgium in the Fall Semester of 2010 and

2011. The authors discuss obstacles to developing a group work culture among social work students.

Chapter Nine is a testament to how much we can accomplish when we encourage an exchange of ideas across borders and oceans. KEG (Keys to Emotional Growth) Cards were developed by Dr. Eleanor Avinor, a faculty member at the University of Haifa in Israel; they are a therapeutic tool for helping clients to move more easily through denial and resistance. Willa J. Casstevens, a North Carolina, USA academic/practitioner, provides her insights on the power of KEG Cards in group work, including their invaluable use as a tool within therapeutic and psycho-educational and groups.

Chapter Ten provides an exciting new feature offered in a Proceedings volume. Long Island Symposium attendees were impressed by the scholarship and sophistication of the event's poster presentations. We felt it worthwhile to include brief summaries of some of these presentations in a chapter of this volume. For this chapter we selected four authors, Jorūnė Vyšniauskytė-Rimkienė, a group worker from Lithuania, and P. Matthew Lozano, Lauren Phillips, and Emily Wilk, group workers from the U.S. Each of their summaries in this chapter represents the spirit of our future IASWG group work scholars.

In *Chapter Eleven*, Ellen Sue Mesbur, a Toronto, Ontario, Canada group work academic and practitioner, provides reflections and memories of IASWG. Weaving together her own IASWG journey with those of other IASWG members, Mesbur surfaces poignant themes of looking back, lessons learned, and looking forward.

The authors of the chapters in this book are group work practitioners in such diverse countries as Lithuania, Israel, Belgium, Canada, Iran, Ireland, and the United States. After reading their work, we hope you will more fully appreciating the complicated, frustrating, surprising, and exciting world of the international group worker.

Gregory J. Tully, Jean Bacon, Georgianna Dolan-Reilly, Alexandra Lo Re

1
Diversity in group work practice:
An obstacle or opportunity?

William Pelech and Robert Basso

Introduction

There is an increasing awareness of the need for culturally sensitive practice today because of the changing demographics in our communities. The changes arising from life in an increasingly globalized world have further reinforced a demand for more inclusive approaches to practice. Diversity has been defined as including differences in demographic characteristics and informational differences. However, there is a curious lack of empirical studies examining how to work with heterogeneous groups, or how to address and explore issues of diversity among group members in a sensitive and effective manner. In multiracial groups, workers have expressed concerns that group members would perceive them as having insufficient understanding of cultural issues and would not participate in discussion due to racial tensions. Most disturbingly, when facing group member differences or working with members from different backgrounds, the most common response from group workers reportedly was that they did nothing. A lack of effective strategies may contribute to the alarmingly high attrition rates in treatment groups. In a meta-analysis of 125 studies, Wierzbicki and Pekarik (1993) reported a mean dropout rate of 46.9%.

This chapter offers a summary of a presentation and discussion at the 2012 Annual Symposium of the International Association for the Advancement of Social Work with Groups. After briefly defining what we mean by diversity for the purposes of this discussion, and a short summary of a related research project, we will examine two vignettes that were presented for discussion at the Symposium as a way of demonstrating how diversity can be used as an opportunity for group development and the achievement of member goals.

Background

Diversity has been generally defined as the state or quality of being different, unlike in character or qualities. Definitions of diversity include ""variety, unlike in nature" (Oxford Dictionary, 2001, p. 276) and "variety, or the opposite of homogeneity" (Barker, 2003, p. 126). Definitions also include descriptions of people from minority populations and people from varied backgrounds, cultures, ethnicity and viewpoints, a common orientation for many human service organizations.

While the usage of the term diversity is more recent, group work practice has always emphasized respect for the uniqueness of each individual and the importance of democratic values in practice. In the 1930's, at a time when group work included professionals from a wide array of disciplines, Coyle realized that member differences bring creative potentials to a group. Many group practitioners since then have also realized the value and creative potential arising from the recognition and integration of differences (Newstetter, 1938; Tropp, 1969; Konopka, 1956; Kaiser, 1958; Goroff, 1980, Kurland & Salmon, 1998, Philips, 1957). Social work is distinctive in its early adoption of an ecosystems theory, which views diversity as a resource for groups. As Balgopal and Vassil (1983) observed, "Group environments which allow the accumulation and expression of differences in individuals facilitate an increase in the alternative choices and behaviors to its members for coping with problems and obtaining need satisfaction" (p. 125-6). Shulman (2006) explicated the dynamics of mutual aid as including diversity oriented features such as dialectic processes (i.e., integrating various points of view) and discussion of taboos. Thus, diversity is a resource for achieving group purposes (Sullivan, 2004). Kurland and Salmon (1998) differentiated between demographic dissimilarities (racial, ethnic, cultural gender or other member characteristics) and differences of opinion or perspectives, which also may arise as a result of diversity in the membership of a group.

Given social work's conceptualization of diversity as including differences in demographic characteristics and informational differences, we will tentatively adopt this more inclusive definition here. Our reason for this definition lies in the complexity of diversity. A group member's identity is simultaneously an individual and group characteristic and a representation of social interaction (Green & Stiers, 2002). Even among members of groups who share a common cultural background, profound differences in perspectives may arise (Christensen, 1986). Thus, "in order to avoid stereotyping, social workers must also recognize that heterogeneity within cultures is as important as diversity between cultures" (Este, 1999).

However, there is a curious lack of empirical studies examining how to work with heterogeneous groups, or how to address and explore issues of diversity among group members in a sensitive and effective manner (Bemak & Chung, 2004; Delucia-Waack & Donigian, 2004; Fluhr, 2005; Frey, 2000; Haley-Banez et al., 1999; Saino, 2003; Smith & Shin, 2008). In multiracial groups, workers have expressed concerns that group members would perceive them as having insufficient understanding of cultural issues and would not participate in discussion due to racial tensions (Davis, Galinsky, & Schopler, 1995). Spurred by these findings Schopler, Galinsky, Davis, and Despard (1996) proposed the RAP model involving (1) recognizing-critical racial, ethnic, and cultural differences in the group, (2) anticipating-how individual members and the group as a whole will be affected by racial issues, and (3) problem-solving-where the leader stops the action, confronts the issue directly and problem solves when there is a problem between persons of different races. However, this model has not been tested with actual treatment groups. Most disturbingly, when facing group member differences or working with members from different backgrounds, the most common response from group workers reportedly was that they did nothing (Rittner, Nakanishi, Nackerud, & Hammons, 1999). A lack of effective strategies may contribute to the alarmingly high attrition rates in treatment groups. In a meta-analysis of 125 studies, Wierzbicki and Pekarik (1993) reported a mean dropout rate of 46.9%.

Findings in organizational and social psychology (McLeod, Lobel, & Cox, 1996; Milliken, Barel, & Kurtzberg, 2003; Watson, Kumar, & Michaelsen, 1993) suggest that informational diversity in groups provides for greater variation in perspectives, enabling group members to develop different approaches for dealing with problems and reach higher quality solutions. Research has shown that multicultural groups can develop better alternatives to a problem than do culturally homogeneous groups (McLeod, et al., 1996). Two studies (Cox, Lobel, & McLeod, 1991; Watson, et al., 1993) found that when comparing ethnically homogenous and heterogeneous groups, between-group differences converged over time, with heterogeneous groups obtaining better outcomes than homogeneous groups, particularly when group members learn to work with one another and value their unique contributions (Allmendinger & Hackman, 1995; Jehn, Northcraft, & Neale, 1999). Many studies also suggest that diversity can be managed productively to improve group outcomes (Kearney & Gebert, 2009; Shin & Zhou, 2007; Somech, 2006; Walsh, Henderson, & Deighton, 1988).

Diversity and Group Development

To develop effective strategies to work effectively with diversity, one must also understand how groups develop over time. Indicating the need for new models, most models of group development were formulated in the 1960's (e.g. Northen, 1969; Tuckman, 1963). One of the most enduring developmental models, the Boston Model (Garland, Jones, & Kolodny, 1965), includes five developmental stages: (1) pre-affiliation-as members enter the group they are acutely aware of their perceived inadequacies and differences. In the absence of information members are likely to fill the void with prior experiences. These potentially negative experiences may further heighten the anxiety of members. Aside from noting that "divergent behavior may have common purposes" (Garland, Jones & Kolodny, p. 30), the model offers little to acknowledge and affirm the value of member differences and to address issues of diversity during this phase; (2) power and control-this stage is characterized by member rebellion and strivings for greater autonomy. Though the worker gives "tacit acceptance of the expression of anti-social feelings" and assures each member "a reasonable degree of safety from attack" (p. 44-45), little is offered in terms of how to work with differences that arise at this point; (3) intimacy-here the group will have successfully negotiated differences arising amongst its membership. Individuals at this stage are encouraged to discuss how their own family experiences relate to present behaviors and relationships. However, family-like bonds may promote member loyalties that may severely limit the expression of differences in the group; (4) differentiation-it is at this point where, finally, "members begin to accept one another as distinct individuals" (p. 52). This implies that acceptance of each member's unique contributions must wait to the later stages of the group. But, as several have observed (Delucia-Waack & Donigian, 2004; Garcia-Coll, Cook-Nobles, & Surrey, 1997), differences between group members should be explored sooner; and (5) separation-as the group comes to an end, members will display different responses as a way of dealing with the pain associated with ending. The more ably individuals handle termination processes in the group, and consolidate their learning, the more likely they will be able to do so outside of the group. However, the model fails to fully articulate how these differential responses may be harnessed in the service of group goals. Contemporary theorists have questioned the appropriateness of these stages for women's groups (Schiller, 2007), institutionalized elderly (Kelly & Berman-Rossi, 1999) and psychiatric groups (Kelly, 2004). Others have emphasized the need to explore differences and taboo issues (DeLois & Cohen, 2000; Malekoff & Laser, 1999; Shulman, 1999), particularly those relating to beliefs associated with diversity, oppression and power (Davis, et al., 1995; Delucia-Waack & Donigian, 2004). In sum, while social work has valued diversity, little has been offered in terms of practice strategies that help realize its promise to respond to dramatic societal changes. Given this context, identifying these elements of diversity and generating evidence-based practice strategies are integral to maximizing the potential impact of group work.

Pilot Study Findings

To address the limited research available on this topic, the authors conducted a pilot study to examine how experienced group work practitioners worked with diversity in their groups from pre-group planning to endings. As a separate report of the findings of this study is presently under review, we will incorporate a brief summary here. The pilot study included a purposive sample of 14 experienced group work practitioners from a variety of disciplines (8-social workers, 2-pastoral counsellors, & 4-psychologists) working with a variety of groups in the Calgary & Niagara regions of Canada. They were asked to respond to questions regarding how they viewed diversity and worked with it over the life of their groups. Included in the sample were eight women and six men, twelve of which were Caucasian and two were African-Canadian.

Pre-group

At the pre-group phase, in relation to diversity among the worker, some viewed a Diversity orientation as representative – that an agency should have representative staff members of different cultural, ethnic or racial groups to serve clients like themselves. Some viewed a Diversity orientation as proactive – that agencies might hire sensitive group workers who would be able to assist group members from many different backgrounds. However, in terms of group recruitment, diversity was not "used" in developing group inclusion criteria. Thus, despite the diverse methods used in recruiting, diversity does not directly impact the final group composition.

Creating Safety

For group members, entering a room with a group of strangers for the first time can be intimidating. There is also a certain amount of nervousness about what the group process will actually be like. It is at this stage of the group where awareness and sensitivity to diversity is most prominent. Every group member already has their own unique ways of being, unique patterns of behaviour and unique expectations of group. One major group task is to create a safe environment for the members to feel relaxed and more open about sharing of themselves and their stories so that they can maximize their participation in group.

Emergence of Pro-diversity Norms

Through the connections arising from shared presenting problems/ issues, the unique experience of each member, as well as creation of a safe space where the worker affirms the indispensible and unique contributions that each member can make to the group, the group will naturally create pro-diversity norms which will enable it to help members to achieve their own personal goals for group, achieve group goals as a whole and help develop new ideas for problem solving. As one respondent indicated, ""*So it wasn't tryin to change people's belief systems. It was about challenging themselves to see themselves and others in a different way.*" Group workers also perceived a challenge and a responsibility in diverse groups to balance the goals of the group with the individual goals of group members.

Below is the first of two vignettes presented at the Symposium. The setting is an inpatient psychotherapeutic group in a residential mental health program. This 12 week group has 8 members, with a mixed membership of 4 males and 4 females which has met for four prior sessions. The group is intended to help members to explore the meaning and effects of depression and anxiety in their interpersonal relationships and social functioning within the group and in their daily lives. Symposium participants were asked to read the vignette, and then report how they would respond as the group worker.

> Over several of the past four sessions, group members have shared their struggles with depression and how it has impacted their lives. Tony and Roy have shared the steps that they have taken in trying to fight off its effects. Stating that they will never give in. Others have noted how it has been difficult, but they have tried to take small steps. Up to this point the group has been supportive of their mutual efforts and challenges. One member, Cindy has repeatedly described how she has been victimized by her illness. Cindy feels that no one (e.g., parents, partner) can understand how she feels and she feels powerless to change herself and her life. Next, Roy and Tony repeatedly offer suggestions to Cindy to help her deal with some of the problems that she has shared. In response Cindy states that she appreciates their suggestions, but that she doesn't think that what they have offered is helpful. She continues to share her victimization, and later in response, Roy says "Does anyone have a violin?"

As one might anticipate, often the response by participants is to reinforce group norms at this point by indicating to Roy that his response served to invalidate Cindy and to have him restate it in another more respectful fashion. Such a response would promote pro-diversity norms. However, as the group moves into the middle phase, one could work with diversity at a much deeper and therapeutic level. For those who experience depression, there is often an inner critical voice that serves to attack the self-worth of those who are affected. There is often a profound sense of hopelessness and despair that those with depression experience. The voices present in the group at this time reflect the inner voices that each member experiences. Roy presented the critical voice and Cindy presented the voice of hopelessness. Engendered socialization may also have played an important role. For men like Roy, the voice of hopelessness and powerlessness is often intolerable. The worker here can play an important therapeutic role by not only asking Roy to re-phrase his statement, but to explore what he and others in the group are experiencing as they hear Cindy's story. In doing so, they may begin to come to grips with their stories of victimization. The worker may also explore with Cindy and other group members the impact of Roy's statement and encourage them to assert their feelings to say "no" to the critical voice in the group. In this fashion, diversity can be utilized for profound therapeutic effect.

Middles

Provided the necessary therapeutic conditions of respect for diversity and psychological safety have been achieved, the group may become a more effective agent of mutual aid and individual change. During this stage, group members fully realize the value of diversity and the importance of each group member's unique contributions and efforts towards individual and group goals. Here, members are able to be close and yet different. Built into the group process are commonalities in terms of presenting issues that brings group members to the same place at the same time, and that can facilitate a common point of connection at the beginning of group. Thus, diversity is used to facilitate an ebb and flow between uniqueness of the group members and the cohesion and sense of connection between members. Members come to realize that even with their separateness they can empathize with each other and to provide realistic feedback to each other and the worker. Moreover, each of them can use their differences to find new interpretations of the problem, and by extension, new ways of resolving problems. Members at this point are able to accept and use the problem-solving method to deal with problems in and out of the group. Among the stages of group development this stage has the greatest potential for individual change.

The safety and trust developed earlier also encourages members to try out new behaviors while relating. Other members are quick to give honest and realistic feedback in sensitive and caring manner. Challenge is counter-balanced by support. Clarifications are sought and are often readily given. In this way, the individual's treatment goals may be achieved with group support, and the group may achieve one of its primary objectives, namely individual change through the group process. Often, during this stage, there is excitement about personal achievements and about the achievements of others. Interdependence is highlighted, while dependence is minimized. There is a need to see others as they are and to accept their uniqueness. As noted in the above vignette, Tony and Roy could be encouraged to explore their experiences of victimization and Cindy could be supported in saying no to critical voices.

While the worker will adopt a more peripheral position at this stage as the group tends to run itself, he or she plays a pivotal role in the transition from the previous stage. As the interactions unfold around differences, the worker facilitates mutual empathy among members and continues to reinforce the value of diversity and acknowledge the importance of each group member's unique contributions and efforts towards individual and group goals. It is through the unique contributions of individuals that members gain personal insights into their own situations. With the awareness gained, members can be challenged by each other and the practitioner to change their ways of thinking, feeling and behaving. The practitioner also assists with the clarification and interpretation of the process as it unfolds, and can also expect that the discussion or activity during this stage would revolve around the themes of identity and interdependence. The worker can also help members to normalize their feelings of ambivalence regarding the proposed change, then to realistically evaluate the advantages and disadvantages of the change and to take action in keeping with their treatment goals.

As the member tries out new behaviors while relating, other members are quick to give honest and realistic feedback in sensitive and caring manner. Members can be taught to challenge other members whose feedback is overly critical and given in an uncaring manner, because when the feedback is given in a sensitive and helpful manner, individuals are able to accept it, and this in turn will reinforce the desired behaviors. In this way, the individual's treatment goals may be achieved with group support, and the group may achieve one of its primary objectives, namely individual change through the group process.

Not only are members encouraged to try new behaviors in the

group, but they are encouraged by each other and the worker to take their insights and learning from the microcosm of the group into the macrocosm of their larger social environments. Members are encouraged to examine all aspects of their social and personal relationships, and at the same time look at other relationships outside of the group. There must be support and encouragement for trying new behaviors outside of the group and seeking the group's response to these efforts after they have been tried. Such support and encouragement serves in heighten constructive criticism between and among members.

Endings

Finally, as the group moves into and through this stage, members will begin to realize that the group is not going to last forever and will begin to express concern over its ending. These concerns herald the onset of the final stage in the group. As the group comes to an end, members will display different responses as a way of dealing with the pain associated with ending or loss. These responses have been identified as flight, denial, regression, a need to continue, recapitulation and review and evaluation (Garland, Jones and Kolodny, 1965).

In our final vignette, we present a 12 week support group for women who have experienced domestic violence. Again, Symposium participants were instructed to read the vignette and then offer their feedback on what they would respond as a group worker:

Over the past weeks the members of the group have developed really close ties. Many have shared experiences and secrets with other group members that they had never told anyone else. From the isolation of an abusive relationship, many of the members have really felt unconditional support and acceptance for the first time in years. There have been many tears and angry words at times, but members feel that no matter what their group will be there for them. Tonight is the 10th meeting, near the end of the meeting, the group worker, asks for feedback on member's experience in the group. During recent weeks members have expressed their appreciation for the support that they have felt in the group. Tonight everyone offers similar feedback except for Sally who shares:
"You know the group is not that great. I mean, don't get me wrong,

I have learned some things but it's not the same as it was for me.
Besides, it's going to end and then what?"
After Sally share her feelings and thoughts, group members challenge
her on why she feels this way. They also attempt to re-assure her that
they will continue to be there to support her after the group ends.

The response of the group members here, may also reflect a response
that a worker who adopts a more defensive stance with respect to
the group might undertake. However, a more inclusive approach to
diversity requires a different approach. Through accepting and working
with these diverse responses the worker too can help group members
acquire a deeper, more balanced and realistic appraisal of the meaning
of their group experience. Such a valuing of diversity can be challenging
for both the worker and group members. For example, respecting
diversity at this point may also involve accepting and exploring negative
comments and member disenchantment. Where the practitioner or
group members react defensively or allows punitive responses to such
differences, he or she impairs the group's ability to realistically appraise
the achievement of individual and group goals and to gain insight
into the personal meaning of the ending for each member. Indeed, by
dismissing negative appraisals or feelings an important therapeutic
opportunity is lost.

The worker primary aim during this stage is to assist members to
put separation in a realistic context and to make connections with the
ending of the group and their own endings in other social situations.
This stage also provides opportunities for members to share their
fears, desires, and concerns so that there is a sense of ending and not
an overwhelming feeling that there is or will be unfinished business.
The more ably individuals handle their terminating processes in the
group and consolidate their learning; the more likely they will be able
to handle similar processes outside of the treatment group.

As groups and individuals anticipate the end of their social
interaction with each other, they often try to re-enact and review in
great detail various parts of the group experience from earlier sessions
(Garland, Jones & Kolodny, 1965). This provides an opportunity for the
group leader to ask the group what the specific re-enactment or review
meant; what insights were gained and how these insights may be used
outside of the group. Again, acceptance of diversity will enable group
members to gain additional insights and meanings.

As members reenact and review their experiences, the skilled group
leader can, in an orderly manner, ask the group members to review

their treatment goals, their purposes for entering the group and how they have or have not achieved their goals. If the purposes, goals and objectives are clear, then the evaluative process is much more realistic and significant for all. A crucial aspect of evaluation is the opportunity it provides for members to learn how to constructively terminate social interaction with others. Using the agreed on contract as a focal point, all members including the practitioner, can systematically evaluate their achievements and discuss how their experience may be used in the future.

Conclusion

The context of practice has changed in the past half century since the emergence of helpful group models, such as Carl Roger's model or the Boston model. The globalized world has numerous facets that may not fit into models created almost half a century ago. Groups did not then have to cope with as many of the elements of diversity as seen today. Extreme differences now exist at the neighborhood level and these differences of necessity will be reflected in every human group.

The seasoned practitioners from various professional backgrounds had difficulties describing their utilization of diversity in practice. All of the professional group leaders expressed similar struggles with diversity in practice. According to the group leader's inputs, the professions are also wrestling with these issues. Although they recognized that a group member's world views provide a group with some unique opportunities for members to give meanings to their experiences and informs their ways of relating to others (Anderson, 1997), they acknowledged that there is a need for further theoretical development; i.e. the creation of a ``blueprint`` for assisting individuals, group leaders, and human service organizations to deal with diversity and to create successful group development.

As Towle (1965) identified in *Common Human Needs*, people's psycho-social needs are tied to intertwined, diverse and complex life experiences. She advocated that practitioners attend to assisting the clients to work together in order to achieve their common human needs. In sum, it would appear that some of the early assumptions about the importance of homogeneity and commonalities in group work which underpin our early group practice models may only offer partial direction to group workers today. The harnessing of diversity may need to be developed earlier in the life of a group. As DeLucia-Waak and Donigian (2004) have observed, perhaps real cohesion arises out of shared experiences among group members, and that the differences between group members should be explored sooner.

References

Allmendinger, J., & Hackman, J. R. (1995). The more, the better? A four-nation study of the inclusion of women in symphony orchestras. *Social Forces,, 74*, 423-460.

Anderson, J. (1997). *Social work with groups: A process model.* New York: Longman.

Balgopal, P., & Vassil, T. (1983). *Groups in social work: An ecological perspective.* New York: Macmillan.

Bemak, F., & Chung, R. C. (2004). Teaching multicultural group counseling: Perspectives for a new era. *Journal for Specialists in Group Work, 29*(1), 31-41.

Christensen, C. P. (1986). Cross-cultural social work practice: Fallacies, fears and failings. *Intervention, 74*, 6-15.

Cox, T. H., Lobel, S. A., & McLeod, P. L. (1991). Effects of ethnic group cultural differences on cooperative and competitive behavior on a group task. *Academy of Management Journal, 34*, 827-847.

Davis, L., Galinsky, M., & Schopler, J. (1995). RAP: A framework for leadership of multiracial groups. *Social Work with Groups, 40*(2), 155-165.

DeLois, K., & Cohen, M. B. (2000). A queer idea: using group work principles to strengthen learning in a sexual minorities seminar. *Social Work with Groups, 23*(3), 53-67.

Delucia-Waack, J., & Donigian, J. (2004). *The practice of multicultural group work.* Belmont, CA: Brooks/Cole.

Este, D. (1999). Social work and cultural competency. In G.-Y. Lie & D. Este (Eds.), *Professional social service delivery in a multicultural world* (pp. 27-45). Toronto: Canadian Scholars' Press.

Fluhr, T. (2005). Transcending differences: Using concrete subject-matter in heterogeneous groups. *Social Work With Groups, 27*(2), 35-54.

Frey, L. R. (2000). Diversifying our understanding of diversity and communication in groups: Dialoguing with Clark, Anand, and Roberson (2000). *Group Dynamics: Theory, Research, and Practice, 4*(3), 222-229.

Garcia-Coll, C., Cook-Nobles, R., & Surrey, J. L. (1997). Building connection through diversity. In J. V. Jordan (Ed.), *Women's growth in diversity: More writings from the stone center* (pp. 176-198). New York: The Guilford Press.

Garland, J., Jones, H., & Kolodny, R. (1965). A model for stages of development in social work groups. In S. Berstein (Ed.), *Explorations in group work* (pp. 17-71). Boston: Milford House. (Reprinted from: 1973).

Green, Z., & Stiers, M. J. (2002). Multiculturalism and group therapy in the United States: A social constructionist perspective. *Group, 26*(3), 233-246.

Haley-Banez, L., Brown, S., Molina, B., D'Andrea, M., Arrendondo, P., Merchant, N. (1999). Association for specialists in group work principles for diversity-competent group workers. *Journal for Specialists in Group Work, 24*(1), 7-14.

Jehn, K. A., Northcraft, G. B., & Neale, M. A. (1999). Why differences make a difference: A field study of diversity, conflict, and performance in workgroups. *Administrative Science Quarterly, 44*, 741-763.

Kearney, E., & Gebert, D. (2009). Managing diversity and enhancing team outcomes: The promise of transformational leadership. *Journal of Applied Psychology, 94*(1), 77-89. doi: 10.1037/a0013077

Kelly, T. B. (2004). Mutual Aid Groups for Older Persons with a Mental Illness. *Journal of Gerontological Social Work, 44*(1/2), 111-126.

Kelly, T. B., & Berman-Rossi, T. (1999). Advancing Stages of Group Development Theory: The Case of Institutionalized Older Persons. *Social Work with Groups, 22*(2/3), 119-138.

Malekoff, A., & Laser, M. (1999). Addressing difference in group work with children and young adolescents *Social Work with Groups, 21*(4), 23-34.

McLeod, P., Lobel, S., & Cox, T. (1996). Ethnic diversity and creativity in small groups. *Small Group Research, 27*(2), 248-264.

Milliken, F., Barel, C., & Kurtzberg, T. (2003). Diversity and creativity in work groups. In P. Paulus & N. B. (Eds.), *Group creativity: Innovation through collaboration* (pp. 32-62). New York: Oxford University Press.

Northen, H. (1969). *Social work with groups.* New York: Columbia University Press.

Rittner, B., Nakanishi, L., Nackerud, L., & Hammons, K. (1999). How MSW graduates apply what they have learned about diversity to their work with small groups. *Journal of Social Work Education, 35*(3), 421-431.

Saino, M. (2003). A new language for groups: Multilingual and multiethnic group work. *Social Work With Groups, 26*(1), 69-82.

Schiller, L., Yael. (2007). Not for Women Only: Applying the Relational Model of Group Development with Vulnerable Populations. *Social Work with Groups, 30*(2), 11-26.

Schopler, J. H., Galinsky, M. J., Davis, L. E., & Despard, M. (1996). The RAP model: assessing a framework for leading multicultural groups. *Social Work with Groups, 19*(3/4), 21-39.

Shin, S. J., & Zhou, J. (2007). When is educational specialization heterogeneity related to creativity in research and development teams? Transformational leadership as a moderator. *Journal of Applied Psychology, 92*, 1709-1721

Shulman, L. (1999). *The skills of helping individuals, families, groups, and communities.* Itasca, Illinois: F. E. Peacock Publishers.

Shulman, L. (2006). *The skills of helping individuals, families, groups, and communities* (5th ed.). Milton, CA: Thomson-Brooks/Cole.

Smith, L. C., & Shin, R. Q. (2008). Social privilege, social justice, and group counseling: An inquiry. *Journal for Specialists in Group Work 33*(4), 351-366.

Somech, A. (2006). The effects of leadership style and team process on performance and innovation in functionally heterogeneous teams. *Journal of Management,, 32*(132-157).

Sullivan, N. (2004). Conflict as an expression of difference: A desirable group dynamic in anti-oppressive social work practice. In C. Carson, A. Fritz, E. Lewis, J. Ramey & D. Suguichi (Eds.), *Growth and development through group work* (pp. 75-89). New York: Haworth Press.

Towle, C. (1965). *Common Human Needs.* New York: National Association of Social Workers.

Tuckman, B. (1963). Developmental sequence in small groups. *Psychological Bulletin*(63), 384-399.

Walsh, J., Henderson, C., & Deighton, J. (1988). Negotiated belief structures and decision performance: An empirical investigation. *Organizational Behavior and Human Decision Processes,, 42*, 194-216.

Watson, W., Kumar, K., & Michaelsen, L. (1993). Cultural diversity's impact on interaction process and performance: Comparing homogeneous and diverse task groups. *Academy of Management Journal, 36*, 590-602.

Wierzbicki, M., & Pekarik, G. (1993). A meta-analysis of psychotherapy dropout. *Professional Psychology, 24*, 190-195.

2
Examining the relationship between leader behavior and group climate for aggressive adolescents in group intervention: A pilot study

Marisa D. Mahler and Eva Feindler

Introduction

This chapter aims to quantify key process variables, such as engagement and safe climate, within the context of Aggression Replacement Training (ART) with youth. In addition, treatment fidelity was examined in order to gain information concerning treatment implementation of ART. The study described in this chapter aims to add to the literature of group therapy by identifying the influences of process variables in order to better inform group leaders about their implementation. This might then allow for the examination of group process in psychoeducational training and treatment outcomes in order to help maximize gains. Further, this might also allow for a better understanding of training and supervision needs of program trainers.

Background

The high occurrence of adolescent antisocial behavior has serious implications for society. According to the Office of Juvenile Justice and Delinquency Prevention, juveniles have been involved in roughly 25% of violent crimes over the past 25 years. In 2010, juvenile offenders represented roughly 8% of murder offenders. In New York's juvenile justice system, the recidivism rate for juvenile offenders returning to correctional facilities is 80%, higher than the recidivism rates for adult criminals (Louis, 2008). Higher juvenile crime rates demand more of America's tax dollars to pay for a spectrum of services related to youth crime (e.g. police, judges, detention centers, educational programs, etc.).

A large body of research has shown Aggression Replacement Training (ART) to be an effective intervention for working with aggressive adolescents in reducing behavior problems (Holmqvist, Hill, & Lang, 2007; Reddy & Goldstein, 2001; Goldstein et al., 1998). ART is a multi-intervention, which incorporates three types of intervention within a group context: anger control training, skill-streaming, and moral reasoning training. ART is implemented over 10 weeks with one-hour sessions three times a week. The bulk of previous research concerning ART has focused on treatment outcomes (Cefai & Cooper, 2009; Byrne, 2008; Goldstein et al., 2004; Goldstein et al., 1998; Hatcher, et al., 2008) and has failed to examine group processes occurring during intervention sessions.   Despite the popularity of group work, there is still a major deficit in the area of process research. Most of the research in the field focuses on topics, such as: supervision and training of group leaders (Rivera et al., 2004; Maidenberg, 2003), technique (Ward, 2007; Hanna & Hunt, 1999; Weersing, Weisz, & Donenberg, 2002), non-therapeutic groups (Myers, Edwards, Wahl, & Martin, 2007), group therapy as an effective mode of treatment (Dishion, McCord & Poulin, 1999; Kulic, Horne & Dagley, 2004), and assessment/outcome research (Evans, 1998; Nichols-Goldstein, 2001; Viney, Henry & Campbell, 2001; Zayat, 2001; Lamar, 2006; Truneckova & Viney, 2007). The current study will be a valuable addition to the group work literature, which lacks process research on psychoeducational group therapy with a high-risk population.

Methods

Hypotheses

Hypothesis 1: There will be a direct relationship between therapist engagement and safe group climate. It is expected that a high level engagement will be positively correlated with a high level of safe group climate.

Hypothesis 2: There will be a positive correlation between leader behavior and treatment fidelity, with greater leader engagement associated with higher treatment fidelity scores.

Hypothesis 3: There will be a positive correlation between safe group climate and treatment fidelity, with higher safety associated with higher treatment fidelity scores.

Participants

Data for the current study were collected as part of a larger evaluation of the ART treatment program at the Tidewater Regional Group Home Commission (TRGHC) in Portsmouth, Virginia. Data were collected on the agency's clients and staff and sent to the research team. The data used in this study were collected from November 2006 to April 2010 at two sites using the ART program: Lynnhaven (formerly Chesapeake Boys Home), an all-male group facility, and Centerville Home, an all-female group facility.

Participants in the current study included trained agency staff members who served as group leaders for the ART group treatment. Adult participants (n=14) were 4 male and 10 female group leaders working in the two TRGHC group homes. Participants ranged in age from 27 to 50 years old (M= 40.35, SD= 7.50). The leaders were comprised of an ethnically diverse group: 36% Caucasian, 50% Hispanic, and 14% African American. All of the group leaders held a Bachelors degree. The amount of experience of the participants ranged from 1 to 30 years of experience in the field (M = 10.75 SD = 8.19).

Measures

The present study consisted of 14 videotaped ART sessions randomly selected from a larger set of 28 videotaped ART sessions. Nineteen of the sessions were used in previous research studies to assess treatment fidelity (Gerber, 2009; Engel, 2009) as part of a larger Tidewater program evaluation.

System for Observing Family Therapy Alliances-Therapist (SOFTA-therapist; Friedlander et al., 2005):

The SOFTA - Therapist is an observer rating scale that assesses the therapeutic alliance and generates four scales: therapist's contribution to engagement, emotional connection, safety and the family's shared sense of purpose. Scales were selected based on the directives for this study and included the therapist's contribution to engagement scale and safety scale. The items were rated by an observer using a Likert-scale ranging from "extremely problematic" (-3) to "extremely strong" (+3).

Treatment Fidelity Checklist (Gerber, 2009):

The current study used coding forms created by Gerber (2009), which reflect the directives outlined for the sessions (e.g., Anger Control Fidelity Checklist, session 2) in the ART manual (Goldstein, Glick, & Gibbs, 1998). Coders rated treatment fidelity using a binomial rating system, in which the coders would indicate whether or not the group leader was adhering to the therapeutic directives outlined in the ART manual during the videotaped session.

Procedure

Coders consisted of two female graduate students enrolled in APA accredited Clinical Psychology doctoral programs. Training was conducted in weekly meetings over the course of a month. Due to the presence of multiple sessions with identical leaders within the data set, coders were able to train with actual ART sessions, which were identical to the actual data set. In addition, coders watched SOFTA training videos to help coders learn how to accurately use the SOFTA. Trainees initially watched training tapes with the investigator, stopping the tapes to discuss target behaviors. After achieving consensus on the items, raters began coding practice tapes independently. Once consensus was achieved, raters began coding the actual data. Each tape was double coded by coders in identical order to eliminate any cohort effects. In addition, in order to prevent observer drift, training continued throughout the coding of the data.

Inter-rater reliability was calculated both during the training and during the actual coding of the data. Intraclass correlations (ICC) were calculated using an average correlation as the criterion for calculation; this was the most appropriate reliability, as the final ratings were comprised by using average rater scores.

Results

When rating videotaped sessions for treatment fidelity, coders reached acceptable inter-observer agreement using Cohen's kappa ($k = .90$). Treatment fidelity scores for each session were obtained by averaging the two coders' ratings. In the current study, videotaped ART sessions fidelity scores ranged from 14% to 80% adherence. During training, ICC for Safety was $r = .79$, and $r =. 89$ for Engagement. Reliability was also measured with percent agreement calculated by analyzing the frequency of rater agreement. There was 75% rater agreement on Engagement and Safety variables for the training videos. The hypotheses were each tested by correlational analyses, specifically Pearson's correlation coefficients.

Therapist engagement and safe group climate

A modest positive correlation was found between therapist engagement and safety ($r =.26$, $P =.37$) such that therapists with higher safety scores show a slight tendency to have higher engagement scores, however the findings were not statistically significant.

Engagement and treatment fidelity

Correlational analyses showed that therapist engagement and treatments fidelity are completely independent of each other ($r=-.093$ $P=.75$). However, these findings were not statistically significant.

Safety and treatment fidelity

Correlational analyses showed that safe group environment and treatment fidelity are slightly negatively correlated ($r= -.15$ $P=.61$), yet not significantly. When the therapeutic environment was not rated as safe, therapists adhered more strictly to the treatment. However, these findings were not statistically significant.

Discussion

The goal of the present study was to expand the process research in the area of psychoeducational group interventions, a topic significantly lacking in the previous literature, and to investigate the relationship between leader behavior, safe group climate and treatment fidelity. The results did not show a statistically significant relationship between any of the process variables. The small sample size may be related to these non-significant findings. The correlations are lower than they might have been had there been more variability in the scores, and perhaps the results would have been more stable with a larger sample size. In addition, The SOFTA presented an inherent methodological limitation of restricted range in having a small 6-point scale (-3 to 3).

There are several potential directions for future research, including conducting an identical study employing the same methodology as the current study but with a larger number of group leaders as participants, or examining multiple sessions with each leader. In addition to observer ratings, future studies should include self-report measures by both group participants and group leaders. It would be fruitful for future research to conduct this study in both residential and non-residential settings.

An interesting area for further research studies would be an examination of other variables that correlate with engagement. For example, research could examine whether leaders who are more engaging are also better at maintaining structure or resolving conflict within the group. By studying process variables associated with engagement one could properly assess group leader abilities and provide better training.

Due to the nature of the ART evaluation, the researchers did not have control over whom the leaders were which resulted in great variability in years of experience ranging from 1 to 30 years. The leader sample was not a homogenous group in terms of competence as relating to fidelity. It is recommended that future research focus on measuring therapist competency. It would be interesting to examine whether differences exist between psychologists and non-psychologist in terms of implementing treatment manuals. There may be significantly less adherence for leaders who received less training in facilitating groups. Methods should be developed to determine competency of leaders such as years of experience, training requirements, receiving on-going supervision and other relevant criteria to ensure that the group leader sample is operationally defined.

Although treatment fidelity has gained more attention, it is still unclear how to best address the issue of non-adherence to treatment. This has implications for training group leaders, including when focusing on how to integrate personal therapeutic style with effective implementation of a manualized treatment. More importantly, the practice of implementation must be standardized as well, or else leaders might not be delivering the same treatment even if they are using identical protocols. A fruitful area for future research would be to examine whether or not therapist implementation styles could be standardized in a similar manner to interventions. In addition, it would be helpful to examine whether there is an optimal therapeutic style that would lead to the most effective treatment outcome.

Conclusion

The current findings are specific to the ART program with adolescent offenders; however, the current study should be replicated with other populations and with different treatment settings, CBT interventions, manualized treatments, age groups, and group leaders. Future research should also examine these process variables in a non-residential setting using a manualized treatment for group therapy with high-risk adolescents.

The goal of the present study was to expand the process research in the area of psychoeducational group interventions, a topic significantly lacking in the previous literature, and to investigate the relationship between leader behavior, safe group climate and treatment fidelity. The small sample size, often characteristic of pilot studies, yielded findings that were suggestive although not statistically significant. It is clear that this is an area that would benefit from further research in identifying key process variables in order to improve the quality of group work with high-risk populations. It is especially relevant in current times when constrictions in funding are a reality for many organizations and facilities, and group work is becoming more prevalent as an efficient and cost-effective way to treat youth. With the rise in popularity of group work, researchers should conduct a close examination of the process of group work to optimize results with high-risk populations and to provide better training and supervision of those implementing the treatment protocols.

References

Cefai, C. & Cooper, P. (2009). *Promoting emotional education: Engaging children and young people with social, emotional and behavioural difficulties.* London, England: Jessica Kingsley.

Dishion, T.J., McCord, J, & Poulin, F. (1999). When interventions harm- Peer groups and problem behavior. *American Psychologist, 54(9),* 755-764.

Engel, E.C. (2009). *Aggression replacement training: Predictors of treatment outcome* (Unpublished doctoral dissertation, Long Island University, C.W. Post Campus).

Evans, J. (1998). *Active analytic group therapy for adolescents. London: Kingsley.*

Friedlander, M.L., Escudero, V., Heatherington, L. (2005). Therapeutic alliances in couple and family therapy. An empirically informed guide to practice. Washington, DC: American Psychological Association Books.

Gerber, M. (2009). *Does gender matter in the treatment of aggressive and antisocial behaviors? An evaluation of a group treatment for high-risk and adjudicated youth* (Unpublished doctoral dissertation, Long Island University, C.W. Post Campus).

Goldstein, A.P., Glick, B., & Gibbs, J.C. (1998) *Aggression Replacement Training: A comprehensive intervention for aggressive youth* (Rev. Ed.). Champaign, Illinois: Research Press.

Hanna, F.J. & Hunt, W.P. (1999). Techniques for psychotherapy with defiant, aggressive adolescents. *Psychotherapy, 36(1),* 56- 68.

Hatcher, R.M., Palmer, E.J., McGuire, J., Hounsome, J.C., Bibly, C.A.L. & Hollin, C. R. (2008). *Aggression replacement training with adult male offenders within community settings: A reconviction analysis. Journal of Forensic Psychology, 19(4),* 517- 532.

Holmqvist, R., Hill, T., & Lang, A. (2007). Treatment alliance in residential treatment of criminal adolescents. *Child & Youth Care Forum, 36(4), 163 -178.*

Kulic, K.R., Horne, A.M., & Dagley, J.C. (2004). A comprehensive review of prevention groups for children and adolescents. *Group Dynamics: Theory, Research and Practice, 8(2),* 139-151.

Lamar, S. (2006). The use of group therapy as a means of facilitating cognitive-behavioural instruction for adolescents with disruptive behaviour. *Australian Journal of Guidance & Counseling, 16(2),* 233-248.

Louis, E. (2008, February 9). Broken juvenile justice system wastes millions of dollars and fails out kids. *Daily News.* Retrieved November 2, 2010, from http://www.nydailynews.com/ opinions/2008/02/10/2008-02-10_ broken_juvenile_justice_system wastes_mi.html.

Maidenberg, M.P. (2003). Considerations in supervision: Conducting child sexual abuse survivor groups. *The Clinical Supervisor, 22(2),* 81-97.

Myers, S.A., Edwards, C., Wahl, S.T. & Martin, M.M. (2007). The relationship between perceived instructor aggressive communication and college student involvement. *Communication Education, 56(4),* 495- 508.

Nichols- Goldstein, N. (2001). The essence of effective leadership with adolescent groups: Regression in the service of the ego. *Journal of Child and Adolescent Group Therapy, 11,* 3-11.

OJJDP Statistical Briefing Book. Online. Available: http://www.ojjdp.gov/ ojstatbb/offenders/qa03105.asp?qaDate=2010. Released on July 31, 2012

Reddy, L.A. & Goldstein, A.P. (2001). Aggression replacement training: A multimodal intervention for aggressive adolescents. *Residential Treatment for Children and Youth, 18(3),* 47-62.

Rivera, E.T., Wilbur, M., Wilbur, J.R., Phan, L.T., Garrett, M.T., & Betz, R.L. (2004). Supervising and training psychoeducational group leaders. *The Journal for Specialists in Group Work, 29,* 377-394.

Truneckova, D. & Viney, L.L. (2007). Evaluating personal construct group work with troubled adolescents. *Journal of Counseling & Development, 85,* 450-460.

Viney, L.L., Henry, R.M., & Campbell, J. (2001). The impact of group work on offender adolescents. *Journal of Counseling & Development, 79,* 373-381.

Ward, D.E. (2007). The challenge of defining techniques in group work. *The Journal for Specialists in Group Work, 32(3),* 207-209.

Weersing, V.R., Weisz, J.R. & Donenberg, G.R. (2002). Development of the therapy procedures checklist: A therapist-report measure of technique use in child and adolescent treatment. *Journal of Clinical and Child Psychology, 31(2),* 168-180.

Zayat, D.B. (2001). Adolescent substance abuse treatment in psychodynamic group psychotherapy. *Dissertation Abstracts International 61*(12B). (UMI No, 6741).

3
Recovering together: Multiple family groups in work with adolescent chemical abusers

Loretta Hartley-Bangs and Colleen Egan

Introduction

This chapter will review the development and implementation of a pilot program in which a multiple family group was introduced into an adolescent chemical dependency intensive outpatient program. The group was modeled on a program facilitated by the Youthdale Psychiatric Crisis Service and the Hospital for Sick Children in Toronto. The facilitators of the Toronto program report "Even when it is not possible to treat youth with a conduct disorder we have found that it is possible to intervene effectively through the parents. Rather than undermine parents' confidence, this therapy strengthens the parents' roles. This approach goes further than merely teaching the parents behavioral methods: it recognizes that the parents have suffered and need support and healing. The group sessions aim to change the parenting style and attitudes of caring, committed parents. Empowerment of parents to deal with antisocial behavior in their children may effectively decrease the incidence of negative behavior in some youth." (Armstrong, Wilks, McEvoy, Russell, & Melville, n.d.) This chapter will address how implementation of these concepts in a multiple family group, within a milieu program for adolescent chemical abusers, can improve program outcomes.

Background

Adolescents who present to chemical dependency treatment programs are often viewed as the "scapegoat" in their family. While the adolescent struggles with their own addiction and behavioral problems, their parents struggle with how to respond appropriately and help their children. The interaction between the adolescent and the parents is often the obstacle to recovery for the child as well as the family, resulting in family role confusion and impaired patterns of interaction and communication.

Parents who bring their children to treatment often present as defensive and fearful of being blamed for the problems of their child. It is necessary to help parents understand family dynamics and to identify the dynamics within their own family to help them learn new ways to respond. Attempts to help the child and family will only be successful if the parents can be engaged in the process. William Madsen (2009) describes this as "Collaborative Helping". His framework is based on 4 commitments: Striving for cultural curiosity and honoring family wisdom; believing in possibilities and building on family resourcefulness; working in partnership with families and fitting services to them; and engaging in empowering processes and making our work more accountable to clients. Madsen's (2009) work is based on the assumption that clients often have abilities, skills, and wisdom that are obscured and unavailable to them. Collaborative Helping and inquiry is a process of joint exploration to elicit those capacities and bring them into constructive use.

While parents need to develop new responses, the adolescent needs to learn how to change their behavior and move out of the scapegoat role within the family. Often the child and their addiction are the catalyst for major positive changes in the family. Providing the opportunity to do this work together as a group allows for greater opportunity for change in all family members. This work is a good fit for what this pilot program was hoping to accomplish. Our goal was to effect change in the adolescent, who was the primary client, through change within the family system.

The multiple family group

Agency context

The North Shore Long Island Jewish Medical Center currently runs an adolescent intensive outpatient treatment program for the treatment of chemical dependency. The average length of stay is 6 months with a step down to "re-entry" which includes 1-2 group sessions weekly, often individual therapy, psychiatric follow up and individual family sessions. Parents are required to attend a 4 week parent orientation group, followed by an ongoing weekly parent group. They are expected to attend group for the length of their child's treatment. All parents undergo a full intake assessment and when necessary are seen in adult services for their own chemical abuse or referred to mental health treatment. Approximately 30% of parents require treatment for their own individual issues.

Over the previous two years the program has experienced a lower rate of completion, even with changes to the program to better accommodate changing family needs and functioning. Approximately 11% of adolescents seen over that two year period successfully completed the program. Forty percent were recommended to residential treatment, with most parents not in agreement. A large percent either left the program or were discharged for noncompliance, usually due to the parents not following the program rules.

What became clear was that we were not doing an effective job of engaging parents. More often power struggles ensued between parents and staff over "following rules". Even in cases where residential treatment was appropriately recommended, often most likely the family would not follow through. Clinical staff observed less movement in treatment and poor communication between themselves and parents who seemed to be struggling with agency expectations regarding supervision of the child outside of treatment hours. Often it became apparent that parents were colluding with the child's negative behavior for fear of consequences for not "following the rules". Not surprisingly, attendance at the parent group was inconsistent and when a parent did inform the staff of a problem or concern, it had been going on for some time. This dynamic interfered with everyone's ability to intervene earlier and to keep the damage down to a minimum.

In an effort to better engage parents and assist families to effect the changes necessary to support their child's recovery, the idea of the Multiple-Family Group therapy was explored. The expectation was that utilizing this modality, in addition to the milieu program for the adolescent and individual family sessions, unhealthy family dynamics and impaired communication patterns could be identified and addressed more quickly. Also providing information to the families about normal adolescent development, communication patterns, family dynamics and the impact of chemical abuse would help normalize each family member's experience and help them learn new ways to interact with each other. Ultimately, we thought, this would enable the family to assist the adolescent chemical abuser in getting clean and sober.

Preparation

In preparation for development of the group, a literature search was done revealing a gap in the amount of research that has been performed with this population. The most extensive evidence-based work was done in a research project in the Midwest by Smith & Hall (2010). While their work employed Multiple-Family Groups as the primary modality for treatment of the adolescent chemical abuser, they came to similar conclusions as we did.

As mentioned earlier, we studied the work of Armstrong et al. (n.d.) in Toronto. While their work was primarily with adolescents diagnosed with a conduct disorder, this was applicable to our population which has a high percentage of adolescents with co-morbid conduct disorders as well as ADD/ADHD and mood disorders. The adolescent and family issues observed by those researchers were similar to what our staff had observed in the IOP (Santisteban & Mena, 2009).

Group process

The pilot was to run for 12 group sessions. The plan was to begin with psycho-education in order to provide needed information on adolescent development, family dynamics and communication, and the impact of chemical abuse. The intent was to provide this information in order to normalize each family member's experience, and to provide a frame of reference. We hoped this would help us engage the parents, as this information would be provided in a non-judgmental way. Once engaged, members would be more open and able to internalize the new information they were receiving. Refocusing everyone's attention on "theoretical concepts" would also serve to take the focus off the scapegoat, the adolescent. In their work with Hispanic family groups, Santisteban and Mena (2009) discussed the importance of psycho-education in work with families. They wrote "Information delivered via psycho educational modules creates "therapeutic frames" for the core presenting problems thereby increasing the family's readiness to achieve the relationship changes they seek" (Santisteban & Mena, 2009). The plan was to gradually move from the more structured groups to less structured sessions in which members felt more empowered and became more active group members. Our belief was that the process of psycho-education would help members engage, leading to group cohesion and allowing for more openness and discussion of individual family issues. Prior to the start of the first session, each member completed a pre-survey which measured parents' confidence in their parental abilities and their assessment of their child's current behavior. This survey was given again later at the 6th session and a post-survey completed following the 12th session. The child's survey measured their sense of their parent's ability to influence their behavior as well as an assessment of their own current behavior.

The twelve sessions were held over a period of fourteen weeks. There were three cancellations, one for a holiday, and two for storms which interfered with the members getting to the agency. We began with three families, one of which dropped out after five weeks due to the mother's employment which did not allow her or her son to continue. The remaining two families each consisted of two parents and one son.

The initial surveys revealed that all the parents gave themselves high ratings in their own abilities. These ratings declined in the six and twelve week surveys for three of four parents. This coincided with declining rates for the behaviors of their children. Each child had relapsed and was eventually referred to residential treatment. The questions this raised for the clinicians included: was this an indication of fatigue and frustration on the part of the parents; were they rating more realistically following the increased communication that took place in the group; how much was attributed to self-blame by the parents ; and were they taking responsibility for their child's regressive behavior?

Group content

An outline of the content in weeks one through four was developed. It covered information in six topic areas. The six topic areas and the information covered in each included: 1) Reviewed group rules and expectations: consistent attendance; commitment to attend for length of child's treatment; no entry after 15 minutes; all cell phones on vibrate; marital issues will be addressed outside of session so as not to involve the child; and ten minutes at beginning of group for "house keeping" issues. 2) Rationale for Multiple Family Group Sessions: mutual support; ability to see dynamics in action; sharing of hope; normalize family dynamics and issues; and decrease shame. 3) Education on Adolescent Brain Development: develops from back to front; frontal lobe is responsible for planning, decision making, impulse control, memory & attention; preference for physical activity; changing sleep patterns; less planning and judgment; impulsive/risk taking; and minimal consideration of negative consequences. 4) Communication: child becomes less communicative; parents become more frustrated; triangle communication; walking on egg shells; communication structures; and family roles (risk and protective factors). 5) Common behaviors seen in adolescent chemical abusers: lying; stealing; threats of violence; withdrawal from family; learning problems; and behavior problems at home, school and in the community. 6) Common behaviors seen in parents of kids who use drugs: feelings of helplessness; depression; guilt/shame; anxiety; feeling overwhelmed; decreased confidence in their ability to parent; and confused and often feel blamed by professionals.

The members initially responded well to the structure. They seemed to welcome the information and the opportunity to have direct communication with their child. Parents were quick to support each other and offer feedback. The first two groups focused on communication. Families began to identify the patterns in their families and provided extensive information through the process of learning. One parent, who was initially resistant to treatment, shared that he felt family dinners were important, but that they rarely happened in his house due to everyone's conflicting schedules. Most members identified with him and took on the challenge of having one family meal over the course of the next week. All members were excited, including the adolescents, two of whom offered to prepare the meal if everyone committed to attending. The group then brainstormed scheduling ideas in order to accomplish this goal (striving for cultural curiosity and honoring family wisdom.)

By the next session only one family had accomplished this goal, however, it led to a discussion of family dynamics illuminated by the process of trying to schedule the family meal. This was an ongoing theme throughout the fourteen weeks. By the end of the program, each family had achieved the goal and continued to try to have at least one family meal per week on some weeks (believing in possibilities and building on family resourcefulness.) This process led to a discussion of the following issues: family roles; family organization; individual feelings; avoidance issues; intimacy issues; the role of each individual in relation to the family's ability or inability to enjoy a meal together; finding a conduit to observe their families; discovering a less threatening way to explore family dynamics.

Outcomes of the multiple-family group

We learned:

- All parents will come in feeling defensive. Clinicians need to engage parents and not get into power struggles with them. The goals should include empowerment.
- Communication patterns can vary among families but there are commonalities.
- Communication between family members has a direct impact on progress, or lack of it.
- Collaboration with the family is necessary to engage all members in the process as well as in treatment planning.
- All families have strengths and things that have worked in the past. These strengths need to be respected and pointed out.

Our beginning hypothesis included the idea that parental attendance in group would improve in a multiple family group setting. With this particular group we saw noteworthy improvement in one family. Compared to previous groups of parents, this group saw improved attendance.

Some issues were identified: Two of the five (40%) parents in the group were identified as having their own substance problem. This was identified at time of the child's intake, and each parent was recommended for their own treatment. One parent appeared resistant initially by her inconsistent attendance at her own treatment sessions. She identified transportation as an issue in her attendance but was able to locate treatment closer to home and gave permission for agency-to-agency collaboration. Reports received showed an ability to abstain which initially coincided with her improved attendance in the multiple-family group. The other parent initially agreed to his own treatment, but also attended inconsistently. His overall attendance improved while attending the multiple-family group.

Of the three adolescents attending, two were referred to residential treatment. This was not seen as a failure, but more related to increased effective communication which allowed the parents to see, more realistically, the struggles of their child. In a more collaborative way, staff was able to work with the family on the referral, resulting in admission and engagement in residential treatment. Part of the work with the parents was to help them see this need for more intensive treatment not as a failure, but as a necessary step to help the child obtain sobriety.

Both sets of parents remained in the group until their child was admitted to the residential program and were engaged in the family program of that agency. One parent has remained in our agency for his own treatment for substance abuse. Both have provided updates on their children who remain in residential treatment successfully.

Discussion

Work with families is more effective when done in a collaborative fashion. Clinicians need to recognize and respect the strengths of all family members, and the difficulty in seeking help which involves exposing the family functions, roles, etc. In attempting to help the adolescent, this collaboration also needs to include other systems involved, such as school, PINS diversion/PINS, probation, etc. All agencies involved need to be recognized as part of the team that is working for the betterment of the child and family.

While all families are unique, common communication patterns and dynamics are seen. We utilized Peter Laqueur's communication style as a starting point for discussion. This included several descriptive factors addressing:

1. Communication: superficial- everyone is turned off by everyone else, and they do not talk about anything but superficial issues; control tower- all communication goes through one person, such as in triangle communication; sex gap- little communication between sexes; generation gap- parents communicate with each other, kids communicate with each other, but the parents and kids don't communicate with each other; scapegoating- one or two family members are accused of causing all the problems.
2. Family Dynamics: symbiosis- mother and son or father and daughter are locked in a symbiotic relationship, producing jealously and alienation of other family members; in-laws- mother or father has too intense a relationship with his or her own parents, leaving their spouse to feel less important; members are too involved in outside interests; and difference in value systems- within important economic, racial, religious, philosophical differences and different cultural and social customs. (Laqueur, n.d.).

If the parents have not resolved roles prior to the birth of their children these dynamics will continue and impact the family functioning. When these concepts were presented, family members quickly became engaged in discussing their own family. We attributed this to families internalizing objective information that related to them, thus giving them words to identify what was going on. Understanding these dynamics and patterns made them feel less unique , and thus less at fault for what was going on in the family and with their child. For the identified client, the adolescent, this began the process of removing them from the role of scapegoat. In working more closely with the families in this modality, it was easier to identify the patterns and dynamics that the adolescent was responding to, thus offering more opportunity to intervene.

For the clinicians who had previously worked primarily with the adolescent, working in this modality offered a different view of the parents. Prior to this, parents were often viewed as an obstacle to the child's progress in treatment. Often power struggles ensued between staff and parents regarding setting limits, follow up etc. While further studies with larger numbers are needed to validate this, it indicates that this way of working may better engage the families as evidenced by the ability to determine a different course of treatment for the child and better follow through.

Summary

The field of substance abuse has long known that addiction is a "family disease". Everyone is impacted and the disease runs through generations. What has been less studied is how to intervene with the families beyond acknowledging the commonly seen roles and impaired communication patterns. What this pilot taught us is the effectiveness of group work with families when it is done in a way that is respectful of the family's culture, wisdom and history. In addition we need to recognize that all family members need help in making changes, not just the chemical abuser.

References

Armstrong, H., Wilks, C., McEvoy, L., Russell, M., & Melville, C. (n.d.). *Group therapy for parents of youths with a conduct disorder.* Retrieved from: http://www.counsellingassociates.com/cmaj.htm.

Laqueur, H.P. (n.d.). *Structures of Disturbed Families.* Retrieved from http://www.mutiplefamilygrouptherapy.com)

Madsen, W. C. (2009). Collaborative Helping: A Practice Framework for Family-Centered   Services. *Family Process*, 48 (1),103-116.

Santisteban, D. A., & Mena, M.P. (2009). Culturally Informed and Flexible Family-Based Treatment for Adolescents: A Tailored and Integrative Treatment for Hispanic Youth. *Family Process*, 48 (2), 253-268.

Smith, D. C. & Hall, J. A. (2010). Implementing Evidence-Based Multiple-Family Groups with Adolescent Substance Abusers. *Social Work with Groups*, 33(2-3), 122-138.

4
Effects of peer group intervention on sexual addiction treatment in Iran

Masoomeh Maarefvand
and Maryam Sadat Mirmalek Sani

Introduction

This chapter looks at a research study conducted with members of Sexaholics Anonymous (SA) in Iran, and investigates the effects of participating in 12-step peer group counseling on abstaining from sexual addiction and other related factors. Three hundred and ten sexual addicts (293 male and 17 female) participated in the study. Just 4% of participants were referred to peer groups by specialists. About 74% had sought substance or alcohol abuse treatment before. Masturbation (86.5%), voyeurism (63.9%), multiple sexual partners (55.2%) were reported by participants as their main problems. In addition, 31% of participants reported homosexuality as a main concern for them personally.

The study described in this chapter suggests that consistent participation of *sexual* addicts in peer groups can be effectively helpful in their treatment. Retention rates of sexual addicts who participated in the peer group meetings regularly, and those who were married, were significantly more than those who participated in peer group meetings irregularly and were single. Finally, substance abuse and its treatment have been the most important challenges in Iran for decades. although co- morbid addictions for those with sexual addiction could have effects on group attendence and abstinence, there is no specific plan to treat them. This study highlights how participation of sexual addicts in peer group can be effectively helpful in their treatment.

Background

Sexual problems such as sexual addiction are neglected in many cultures, including in Iran, because sexuality is viewed as a taboo topic by many. Such neglect can lead to restricted efforts in treatment. Limited research suggests various treatments for sexual addiction such as family therapy (Bird, 2006) with an emphasis on a systematic family therapy approach (Phillips, 2006), and long term group therapy (Hook, Hook, & Hines, 2008). Participating in 12-step group meetings of Sexaholics Anonymous (SA) as a part of an individual's treatment plan is also highlighted as beneficial (Cavaglion, 2008a; Cavaglion 2008b ; Parker & Guest, 2003).

In Iran, there has been no research conducted on sexual addiction, and no certain attempts for its definition. There is also no certain treatment protocol for sexual addiction in Iran, and many therapists are not familiar with how to diagnosis and treat the disease. If the prevalence of sex addiction is considered at a minimum level in Iran, more than 2 million people are faced with sexual addiction in the country and few of them will use the scattered treatment programs in psychiatry clinics.

Sexual addiction

Behavioral addiction, even without substance abuse, can disturb life in different facets and lead to considerable difficulty in social, familial and individual performance. Main behavioral addictions include: gambling addiction, eating addiction, internet addiction, computer game addiction and sexual addiction. Sexual addiction was used by Carnes in 1989 for the first time to describe a pattern of out-of-control sexual behavior. He introduced ten signs for sexual addiction, as follows: a pattern of out-of-control sexual behavior; severe consequences due to sexual behavior; inability to stop despite adverse consequences; persistent pursuit of self-destructive or high-risk behavior; ongoing desire or effort to limit sexual behavior; sexual obsession and fantasy as a primary coping strategy; increasing amounts of sexual experience because the current level of activity is no longer sufficient; severe mood changes around sexual activity; inordinate amounts of time spent in obtaining sex, being sexual, or recovering from sexual experience; and neglect of important social, occupational, or recreational activities because of sexual behavior (1991, p.12). Carnes (2001) estimated the prevalence of sexual addiction at approximately 3 to 6 percent of society.

Furthermore, Schneider (1991) recognized three characteristics for sexual addiction; compulsivity, continuation of sexual behavior despite negative consequences, and sexual obsession. Moreover, a need for greater sexual intensity, cravings for sexual activity, denial, withdrawal, secrecy, and mood fluctuations (Cooper & Lebo, 2001; Crawford, 1990; Pincu, 1989), as well as isolation, poor social connections and spending large amounts of hours obtaining sex (Chaney & Blalock, 2006) have been mentioned as symptoms of sexual addiction. Kwee, Dominguez, and Ferrell, (2007) believe that an increasing number of clinicians and researchers recognize the presence of a syndrome marked by compulsive and addictive sexual behavior that affects a portion of the population. Some researchers believe that these symptoms can fall under the titles of sexual obsessive-compulsive behaviors, problematic hyper sexuality, sexual impulsive, sexual dependency or such expression (Gold & Heffner, 1998; Reid, & Carpener, 2009).

There are common traits of sexual addiction which have been reported in research. For example, high risk behaviors have been reported in sexual addiction (Kalichman & Rompa, 1995, 2001; Smolenski, Ross, Risser, & Simon Rosser, 2009; Grov, Parsons, & Bimbi, 2010), and high prevalence of sexual addiction has been shown in specific groups such as individuals afflicted by HIV/AIDS (Muench, et al., 2007; Kingston & Firestone, 2008; Kalichman & Rompa, 1995, 2001; Grov, Parsons, & Bimbi, 2010) and sexual offenders (Marshall & Marshall, 2006).

Giugliano (2008) concluded that high levels of sexually impulsive behaviors may show addictive behavioral patterns in other areas of life. In the survey that was conducted by Carnes (1991) on 289 sexual addicts, less than 17 percent of respondents reported only sexual addiction. Dual addiction included; chemical dependency (42 percent), eating disorder (38 percent), compulsive working (28 percent), compulsive spending (26 percent) and compulsive gambling (5 percent). Raymond, Coleman, & Miner (2003) reported 71% prevalence of substance abuse among individuals afflicted by problematic hyper sexuality. Not treating sexual addiction may lead to relapse in treating alcohol or substance addicts (Williams, 1999).

Interestingly, people who experience co-morbid addictions like chemical and sexual addition often make this striking observation: chemical abuse is easier to stop than sexual addiction (Carnes, 1991, p.34). Finally, it is essential to note that usually high risk behaviors link sexual addiction to other social problems. In sexual addiction, problems not only affect addicts but also their family, sexual partners, work environment and social relations seriously (Schaeffer, 2009; Peck, 2002; Carnes, 2001). Despite the amount of research conducted on both sexual addiction and co-morbid addiction in sexual addicts, there is no standard suggested treatment protocol for these populations.

Sexaholics Anonymous in Iran

In Iran, the Sexaholics Anonymous Association was established in 2003 in Shiraz. According to records declared by the Association, without awareness of any other Sexaholics Anonymous groups throughout the world, it's founding members decided to abandon their concupiscence and used the 12-step structure of Alcoholic Anonymous to focus on addressing their sexual addiction with a meeting once a week. Later, they found that such an association existed globally. Sexaholics Anonymous Association in Iran has since developed gradually and today has 2000 active members active in 10 provinces of Iran. Females constitute less than 5% of members and participate in special, and separate, female meetings.

The 12-Steps and other traditions of SA constitute the main pillars used in the group to assist with recovery and abstinence, and are used in a self-help pattern. The members of SA believe that attendance in meetings constantly and commitment to the 12-steps and traditions may help them remain in abstinence. This chapter looks at a research study conducted with members of Sexaholics Anonymous (SA) in Iran, and investigates the effects of participating in this 12-step peer group counseling on abstaining from sexual addiction and other related factors.

Study methods

As research questionnaires assessing sexual behavior often request details of past sexual behaviors, and problematic behavior patterns, which could lead SA members to cravings there could often be hesitation in completing questionnaires and participating in research for this population. To avoid this issue, a simple questionnaire was designed with the help of the Iranian Sexaholic Anonymous' Registering Committee, who cooperated to distribute and collect the questionnaires during our data collection phase. Therefore, SA members filled out the questionnaires with less resistance.

Three hundred and ten Iranian SA members (293 males and 17 females), who participated in meetings regularly, answered the questionnaire. For the purposes of statistical analysis, Chi square and T-test used to compare mean age and abstinence and membership duration. Data were analyzed and reported by descriptive statistics, t- test and Pearson correlation coefficient.

Study findings

General demographics:

The mean age of the survey participants was 29 years old, and 30% were reported as married (Table 1). More than 71% of participants supported at least one of the other members of SA as a peer counselor. All participants had worked up to at least the third step out of the 12 steps of SA.

More than 82 percent of participants were acquainted with SA through other members of SA, and specialist referral accounted for less than 4% of first contact. Approximately 74% of participants reported participation in other 12-step groups due to substance or alcohol abuse.

Table 1
Frequency and percentage of demographic characters of participants

Variables		Frequency	Percent
Age (Year)	15-20	31	10.0
	21-30	181	58.4
	31-40	82	26.5
	41-50	13	4.2
	51-63	3	1.0
Marital status	Single	218	70.3
	Married	92	29.7
Gender	Male	293	94.5
	Female	17	5.5
Sponsor/ Peer counselor	No answer	25	8.1
	Yes	223	71.9
	No	62	20.0
Type of first contact with SA	Other SA Members	256	82.6
	SA Website	6	1.9
	Journals of SA	1	0.30
	Physicians or Psychiatrists	12	3.9
	Others	35	11.3
Membership in other 12-step programs	No answer	9	2.9
	Yes	229	73.9
	No	72	23.2

Problematic sexual behavior

Masturbation, fantasy, voyeurism, relations with multiple sexual partners, homosexuality, and abusive sexual relations were the most reported problematic sexual behaviors by participants (Table 2).

Table 2
Frequency and percentage of participants' reported problematic sexual behavior before membership in SA

Reported Problematic Sexual Behaviors	Frequency	Percent
Masturbation	268	86.5
Fantasy	207	66.8
Voyeurism	198	63.9
Multiple Sexual Partners	171	55.2
Homosexuality	96	31.0
Abusive Sexual Relations	50	16.1

T-tests also showed that individuals who reported masturbation, fantasy and voyeurism as their main problems were significantly younger than others who did not report those problems. In contrast, the mean age of participants with abusive sexual relations was higher than others did not report abusive sexual relations (Table 3).

Table 3
Reported problematic sexual behaviors and participants' age

Reported Problematic Sexual Behavior		Age (Mean)	t	p	df
Masturbation	Yes	27.80	-5.023	0.012	308
	No	43.33			
Fantasy	Yes	27.62	-3.428	0.006	308
	No	30.47			
Voyeurism	Yes	27.22	4.648	0.000	308
	No	30.95			
Abusive Sexual Relations	Yes	31.42	3.202	0.002	307
	No	28.00			

Chi squares showed that masturbation (χ^2 =31.85, df=1, P=0.002), fantasy (χ^2 =9.11, df=1, P=0.000), voyeurism (χ^2 = 26.16, df=1, P=0.000) and homosexuality (χ^2 =4.08, df=1, P=0.029) were reported significantly more by single participants. In contrast, those who were married reported more abusive sexual relations (χ^2 =72.53, df=1, P=0.000).

Abstinence

Participants reported 8 months of abstinent on average as well as having approximately 10 lapses in abstinence. Individuals with sponsors remained in abstinence longer and experienced lapses less than others (Table 4).

Table 4
Participants' abstinence duration according to receiving peer group counseling

Variable		Abstinence Duration (Month)	t	p	df
Sponsor and Peer Group Counseling	Yes	9.789	3.969	0.000	308
	No	1.548			

Meanwhile, married members in SA participated in meetings more regularly and thus remain in abstinence longer (Table 5).

Table 5
Participants' membership and abstinence duration according their marital status

Variables		Months (Mean)	T	P	df
Membership Duration	Single	15.80	-2.328	0.005	308
	Married	21.71			
Abstinence Duration	Single	5.70	-3.397	0.000	308
	Married	11.69			

Overall, Pearson correlation coefficient test showed that SA members who participated in 12-step group meetings for longer terms remained in abstinence for longer periods.

Discussion

As it is reported, continuous participation with SA treatment 12-step group meetings can be effective for longer abstinence. In addition, those who are married remained in abstinence for longer periods, and report less problems than singles. It is possible that they are more successful than singles because they are more likely to try to focus on healthy partner sexual relations in a family context. For those who are single, it is possible that their singleness may threaten their treatment for this reason.

It was reported by considerable numbers of participants in this survey that they also abused substances or alcohol as a co-morbid addiction with sexual addiction. They considered substance abuse as a problem, and joined Narcotics Anonymous or Alcoholic Anonymous for treatment. However, entrance to the SA program may suggest that sexual addiction is their other, or possibly underlying, main problem.

There are a few limitations associated with the current study. For example, only Iranian SA members who had consistently participated in SA were involved in the study. Therefore, it is not easy to conclude that this 12-step program is useful for all participants, or to determine the failings of such programs, although remaining in SA can be considered a type of success. Finally, although co-morbid addictions for those with sexual addiction could have effects on group attendance and abstinence, there is no specific plan to treat them. Therefore, more research is recommend to study peer group counseling in order to treat co-morbid addictions.

Conclusion

Peer group counseling is one of the most important treatment methods used worldwide that can play a determinant role in treatment of disease and health promotion. Regardless of the challenging title of sexual addiction, of which there is no agreement on among experts, it appears involvement in peer groups for people who suffer from sexual addition can improve the results of their treatment. Conducting more research on group sexual addiction programs, as well as co-morbid addiction programs, could be useful in determining if, and when, it would be an effective complement to individual sexual and co-morbid addiction treatment.

It seems that unawareness of SA for specialists is one of the main reasons for not referring patient to SA in Iran, despite its suggested benefits. Introducing SA and explaining it's outcomes to specialized teams in addiction and sexual problems treatment settings could improve referrals to this group treatment, and thus provide opportunity for more treatment and abstinence.

References

Bird, N. H. (2006). Sexual Addiction and Marriage and Family Therapy: Facilitating Individual and Relationship Healing Through Couple Therapy. *Journal of Marital and Family Therapy*, 32, 297-311.

Carnes, P. (1991). *Don't Call It Love; Recovery From Sexual Addiction*. Toronto; Bantam Books.

Carnes, P. (2001). *Out of the Shadows*. Minnesota: Hazelden.

Cavaglion, G. (2008a). Narratives of Self-Help of Cyberporn Dependents. *Sexual Addiction & Compulsivity*, 15, 195–216.

Cavaglion, G. (2008b). Voices of Coping in an Italian Self-Help Virtual Community of Cyberporn Dependents. *CYBERPSYCHOLOGY & BEHAVIOR*, 11(5), 599-601.

Chaney, M. P. & Blalock, A. C. (2006). Boredom Proneness, Social Connectedness, and Sexual Addiction Among Men Who Have Sex With Male Internet Users. *Journal of Addictions & Offender Counseling*, 26, 111-122.

Cooper, M., & Lebo, R. A. (2001). Assessment and treatment of sexual compulsivity: A multimodal perspective. *Journal of Social Work Practice in Addictions*, 1, 61- 74.

Crawford, D. (1990). *Easing the ache: Gay men recovering from compulsive behavior*. New York: Dutton Books.

Giugliano, J.R. (2008). Sexual Impulsivity, Compulsivity or Dependence: An Investigative Inquiry. *Sexual Addiction & Compulsivity*, 15, 139–157.

Gold, S.N. & Heffner, C. (1998). Sexual Addiction; Many Conceptions, Minimal Data. *Clinical Psychology Review*, 18, 567-581.

Grov, C., Parsons, J.T & Bimbi, D.S. (2010). Sexual Compulsivity and Sexual

Risk in Gay and Bisexual Men. *Archive of Sex Behaviour*, 39(4), 940–949.

Hook, J.N., Hook, J.P., & Hines, S. (2008). Reach Out or Act Out: Long-Term Group Therapy for Sexual Addiction. *Sexual Addiction & Compulsivity*, 15, 217–232.

Kalichman, S.C., & Rompa, D. (1995). Sexual sensation seeking and sexual compulsivity scales: Reliability, validity, and predicting HIV-risk behavior. *Journal of Personality Assessment*, 65, 586–601.

Kalichman, S.C., & Rompa, D. (2001). The sexual compulsivity scale: Further development and use with HIV-positive persons. *Journal of Personality Assessment*, 76(3), 379–395.

Kingston, D.A., & Firestone, P. (2008). Problematic hypersexuality: A review of conceptualization and diagnosis. *Sexual Addiction & Compulsivity*, 15, 284– 310.

Kwee, Alex W., Dominguez, A.W., & Ferrell, D. (2007). Sexual Addiction and Christian College Men: Conceptual, Assessment, and Treatment Challenges. *Journal of Psychology and Christianity*, 26(1), 3-13.

Marshall, L. E., & Marshall, W. L. (2006). Sexual Addiction in Incarcerated Sexual Offenders. *Sexual Addiction & Compulsivity*, 13, 377–390.

Muench, F., Morgenstern, J., Hollander, E., Irwin, T., O'Leary, A., Parsons, J.T., Wainberg, M., & Lai, B. (2007). The Consequences of Compulsive Sexual Behavior: The Preliminary Reliability and Validity of the Compulsive Sexual Behavior Consequences Scale. *Sexual Addiction & Compulsivity*, 14, 207– 220.

Parker, J., & Guest, D. (2003). Individualized Sexual Addiction Treatment: A Developmental Perspective. *Sexual Addiction & Compulsivity*, 10, 13–22.

Peck, K. T. (2002). Sexual Addiction and the Workplace: A Public Sector Employer's Response. *Sexual Addiction & Compulsivity*, 9:127–138.

Phillips, L. (2006). Literature Review of Research in Family Systems Treatment of Sexual Addiction. *Sexual Addiction & Compulsivity*, 13, 241–246.

Pincu, L. (1989). Sexual compulsivity in gay men: Controversy and treatment. *Journal of Counseling & Development*, 68, 63-66.

Raymond, N.C.; Coleman, E.; Miner, M. H. (2003). Psychiatric comorbidity and compulsive/impulsive traits in compulsive sexual behavior. *Comprehensive Psychiatry*, 44, 370-380.

Reid, R.C., & Carpenter, B.N. (2009). Exploring Relationships of Psychopathology in Hypersexual Patients Using the MMPI-2. *Journal of Sex & Marital Therapy*, 35, 294–310.

Reid, R.C., Carpenter, B.N., & Lloyd, T.Q. (2009). Assessing psychological symptom patterns of patients seeking help for hypersexual behavior. *Sexual and Relationship Therapy*, 24(1), 47–63.

Schaeffer, B. (2009). Sexual Addiction. *Transactional Analysis Journal*, 39(2): 153-162.

Schneider, J. P. (1991). How to recognize the signs of sexual addiction. *Postgraduate Medicine, 90*, 171-182.

Smolenski, D. J., Ross, M.W., Risser, J.M.H., Simon Rosser, B.R. (2009). Sexual compulsivity and high-risk sex among Latino men: the role of internalized homonegativity and gay organizations. *AIDS Care*, 21:42-49.

Williams, W. (1999). The Homeless and Sexual Addiction. *Sexual Addiction and Compulsivity*, 6, 23-29.

5

Under the influence of Katy: foundational contributions of Dr. Catherine P. Papell and other greats

Judith A. B. Lee

This chapter provides the content of the first Catherine P. Papell Invitational Session, given by Reverend Dr. Judith A. B. Lee at the 2012 IASWG Long Island Symposium. It focuses on the influence and contributions of Dr. Catherine P. Papell and other greats.

Introduction

I am honored to speak at the first Catherine P. Papell Invitational Session at Adelphi University. This is where Katy taught as a Professor of Social Work and Director of the Direct Practice Division. Here she became, along with her beloved friend and colleague Beulah Rothman, a beacon and an icon in social work education, enlivening and sustaining the theory and practice of social work with groups. I begin by admitting, with no denial at all, that I am under the influence as I say these words. I am under the influence of Katy Papell whose wisdom about social work and justice throws light on my path as I reflect on her contribution to the profession. Ultimately, I will connect what I have learned from Katy, and some of the other greats of her era, to my own group work theorizing and practice.

I will conceptualize and draw together using words, pictures, and my heart as well as my head. In Katy's conception of how students learn in social work I would be an ACO (Papell, 1978). I lead and learn with my heart, my cognition is very close behind and both move me to operationalize and "do what needs to be done" (Middleman, 1978:16). This latter phrase I borrow from Ruth Middleman, another icon and founding mother of CASWG (the Committee for the Advancement of Social Work with Groups) and ultimately AASWG, along with Katy Papell and Beulah Rothman, in the company of other group work giants and foot soldiers of the time.

In the late 1970's, I was one of those foot soldiers in the struggle to keep group work alive and vital in the profession of social work. I was an Assistant Professor at NYU's School of Social Work who participated in meetings of group work educators, including some of my mentors - Bill Schwartz, Hy Weiner and Al Gitterman and field instructors and practitioners, including Toby Berman-Rossi and Maxine Lynn and others, along with Katy and Beulah who were motivating forces. My first introduction to Katy was in this group although I overlapped with Katy at Wurzweiler's School of Social Work at Yeshiva University, where we both did our Doctoral work. Katy completed her Dissertation entitled *A Study of Styles of Learning for Direct Social Work Practice* and was awarded her Doctorate in 1978, and I would follow in 1980 building upon Katy's findings about how social work students learn (Papell, 1978). My piece of the puzzle would be *Teaching Behaviors for Perceived Relevance* (Lee, 1980).

This is a recollection of that time adapted from a tribute I wrote for Beulah Rothman in *Social Work With Groups* after her untimely death in August of 1990 (1990: xiii, xiv). At the time of writing this recollection I was a Professor at the University of Connecticut, President of AASWG, and a group work consultant and practitioner in a shelter for women and children in Hartford, Conn. Katy was still an institution at Adelphi. I am looking back:

It is the late 1970's, in a New York University brownstone. After a round of bad jokes and coffee, there is a fast and strong dialogue going on about group work education. It sounds loud, angry. Bill Schwartz is the protagonist stating his views categorically as he does. Only a few women are present. Beulah listens and then says, 'Wait a minute, that's a crock of....". She sits on the edge of her seat, her colorful scarf draping shoulder to floor. Soon everyone is in on it. Katy is sitting next to Beulah. Now she is the one to say 'Wait' and take up the argument, thoughtfully and without the peppery language. She is beautiful with her long white hair pulled back in a bun with strands falling in her face, wearing a soft grey dress with a splash of color in a long bright necklace. In typical New York manner she is interrupted but she regains the floor. Everyone is talking, yet hearing one another. One would think the stakes were at least world peace! Alex diplomatically mediates. I remember disagreeing with Beulah on a point. Katy suggested that I 'had something' and asked me to expand on it. The work continued. I remember thinking 'something very special has just happened here. The two women from Adelphi are really something!' There are more of these meetings this year. This is my introduction to Beulah and Katy.

"(About ten years later)...I will not forget a car ride from Connecticut to Queens to deliver Ivor Echols and Beulah to Katy's home for an overnight before an AASWG Board Meeting at a New York City Settlement House. What a great group meeting we had in the car. Ivor told stories of the discrimination she faced growing up black in Oklahoma and Beulah talked about anti-Semitism. Both reflected on social work academia and experiences as women in leadership roles. And we also laughed a lot. What a wonderful close time ensued as we accepted Katy's gracious hospitality and our closeness grew as the group meeting continued. I left late at night with the feeling that it was premature to end the meeting".

It was a feeling of loss that would be reminiscent of the loss of Beulah, of Ivor Echols, of so many of our beloved leaders and friends, and most recently of Jim Garland, who was a special guide for me. I suggest that the friendships that we have forged are no ordinary friendships, but anchors in an often stormy sea, and that which lasts beyond space and time.

Katy and Beulah were friends and colleagues of over forty years, and a complementary balance for one another. Katy, in her tribute to Beulah (1990: vii-viii) described Beulah as a "true leader. She moved naturally into a superordinate position throughout her professional life. She loved life and she loved humankind with all the mishegaas, and she loved the creative challenge of helping people engage with people". In this latter dynamic, Katy and Beulah were very much alike and one inspired the other in their pioneering efforts.

A Motivating force: For the Journal, CASWG/AASWG, and the Symposia

In 1978 I got a baptism of fire in the fine art of writing for journals as Katy and Beulah instructed me in improving an article that I submitted for the new Journal of *Social Work With Groups,* co-founded and co-edited by Katy and Beulah (Lee, 1979). Their launching of this Journal in 1978 was a monumental accomplishment. Through the Journal, later edited by Katy herself, then Roselle Kurland and Andrew Malekoff, and now by Malekoff; the launching of CASWG then AASWG: An International Professional Organization-the name was changed in 1987, (Ramey, 2009) ; and the Symposia-from the first in Cleveland in 1979 through this 34th Symposium we have succeeded in keeping group work alive and well in an ever changing profession.

I remember ambivalent feelings as I trekked from NYU to Adelphi to work on the article with them. It did not matter to Katy and Beulah that this was my third published article. I was a beginner, it was their Journal and perfection was the goal - and it was a good thing that it was. Looking back, I am ever thankful for their teaching. When the 1979 Journal hit the presses, I noted that Katy's daughter Linda also had an article in it on group services with COPD out-patients, and I wondered if Katy also had her write and rewrite and rewrite, as it was something that Katy always did for herself.

When I was elected to Chair CASWG in 1986 and again to another three-year term (from 1989-1991), Katy and Beulah, Ruth Middleman and Charles Garvin (the latter two past chairs) along with John Ramey (the glue that often held it all together), Ruby Pernell (my wonderful Vice-Chair and organizational guide), Marty Birnbaum, Jim Garland, Alex Gitterman, Toby and Peter Berman- Rossi, Joe Lassner and others mentored me in this sometimes difficult role. I was in the company of 'a great cloud of witnesses', who guided and assisted me, and, yes, empowered me. Yet, I always envision Katy's attentive face and thoughtful responses as we sat down to discuss difficult problems.

Ever the scholarly practitioner

When I think of Katy, I think of her accomplishments as a doer, thinker, synthesizer, theoretician, and practitioner extraordinaire. The Wurzweiler ideal doctoral graduate was "the scholarly practitioner" - one who applied thought to practice and used practice to generate theory. Katy is the prototype of this ideal.

Canadian theoretician, and icon in her own right, Norma Lang in dedicating her recent book (2010) to Katy, describes her as "quintessential practitioner, scholar, mentor, guardian, and champion of the practice of social work with groups". Katy continued with her practice into her seventh and eighth decades. In that respect, as I approach my seventh decade, I continue to follow her lead. Her practice in later years was challenging work in an addictions services agency. I know the challenge, because while I still prefer work with children and youth, my work with the homeless has led me to those who struggle with addictions. Katy is my vibrant living example to keep on keeping on with this hard work. She is our example in the unity of theory and practice and in the ongoing battle for social justice. Always a champion for justice, in her eighth decade she was a warrior in the cause of Afghan women, and she still is!

But, most of all, when I think of Katy, I think of beauty and elegance, sensitivity, broad inclusive spirituality, a keen and questioning intellect and compassion. It is Katy as a whole person that we celebrate and she is a spectacular example of what it means to be a wise, good and loving human being. Hers is a life that is outstandingly well lived. She is highly deserving of the Lifetime Achievement Award given by the New Jersey Chapter of NASW on May 7, 2012 where, at 95, she gave a rousing twenty minute response.

We turn now to Dr. Papell's thinking and foundational contributions and their impact on the profession and on my own practice with groups and as an educator.

Social work education

I begin with discussing her doctoral dissertation on styles of learning for direct practice (1978). This is a very important study as it remains one of the few studies in the profession that is focused on the social work student as a learner. It is also important because it developed out of Katy's love for her students and her desire to facilitate their learning. In it she recognized the students' need to be engaged at the thinking-feeling-doing levels of functioning with their clients. Using what she described as a "cognition, information-processing conceptual framework" she defined learning style as "the patterned arrangement of three modes of cognitive activity: conceptual, affective and operational". She developed and administered an instrument called the Self Profile of Learning Styles, the SPLS, to 238 students in the first year of social work study. She found that "students showed strong preference for the Operational mode, even distribution of the Affective mode and low preference for the Conceptual mode" (1978:2). On the other hand both the classroom teachers and field instructors studied preferred the conceptual mode. In noting the disparity, Katy suggested that facilitating learning "may require that teaching behaviors be geared toward the fullest development of these modes" (1978:60).

Katy's study fascinated me as my students also struggled with the same issues. I duplicated her study and the results were consistent: students preferred learning by doing and teachers preferred conceptual activities. While these three 'modes' are patterned uniquely in each of us, and interrelated, students preferred learning by doing. I decided to take the next step Katy suggested and study what teaching behaviors could facilitate learning under these circumstances. Bill Schwartz in 1964 (Berman-Rossi, 1994) and Larry Shulman (1972) studied and conceptualized teaching skills based on the reciprocal/interactionist model that drew upon group work skills and were effective with students. But it was Papell that moved us a step closer to documenting how social work students prefer to learn cognitively. My own findings affirmed that "feeling oriented, supportive, experientially focused interactional teaching behaviors were perceived as most relevant to student learning. Teachers who used mainly lecturing behaviors were found to have the least perceived relevance in fact there was no correlation". Both studies highlighted the importance of paying attention to the processes of learning and teaching in social work education. Notably, the use of group work skills was found relevant in social work learning.

Social Work with Groups

In 1966, Papell and Rothman published a landmark article on "Social Group Work Models -Possession and Heritage" in the *Journal of Education for Social Work* (pp. 66-77). In it they compared and contrasted three leading models "representing discrete streams of the whole": the social goals model of the group work founders, the remedial model associated with Robert Vinter and associates, and the reciprocal model of William Schwartz. The dimensions of knowledge sources, group purpose and goals, type of agency, focus of work, image of group member, types of activities, view of the group, worker's skills, methods used, practice principles, and theory base were discussed for each of these of these models.

Their sharp delineation brought choice, clarity and direction to a generation of social work students. While I was learning, and had an affinity for, the reciprocal model from Bill Schwartz at Columbia from 1967-1969, I was also learning clinical social work in Casework as I was permitted a double major. This was called 'medical model' by Bill and 'remedial' by Papell and Rothman. Assumptions about human nature were different in each one, but not as diametrically opposed as I first thought. I admit that while I learned it easily it has taken me a lifetime to put Schwartz's conception of the group into full practice: "The group is an enterprise in mutual aid, a collection of people who need each other to work on certain common tasks, in an agency that is hospitable." (1961; 1971:7; Berman-Rossi, 1994). The concepts of 'mutual need', 'work', 'commonality', and 'agency function' each took years of practice to understand. The worker's tasks of 'demanding work', 'challenging obstacles', and creating the opportunity for work require a plethora of skills combined with deep empathic understanding. Later, Larry Shulman's elaboration of Schwartz's phases of work and tasks was helpful in teaching students the "how-to" of group work (1984; 1992). Gitterman and Shulman as theorists and editors, and others, have amply illustrated group work in this genre in their popular *Mutual Aid Groups and...the Life Cycle* (1985; 2005). It is interesting to note that Shulman's most recent skills book (2011) is cast as group counseling skills and while it broadens the contexts of group practice it also loses its distinct social work identity.

I was also drawn to the work of my teacher Hy Weiner in the social goals tradition (Weiner, 1964) and attuned to the activist and social change climate of the times. It was during this time that Columbia social work students joined a student strike and Francis Fox Piven was photographed in LIFE magazine climbing out of a window on the main campus. Some of our classes were held off campus and faculty and students together participated in a march on Albany, the State Capitol. l often felt tension as if I had to choose between the three models, but the legitimacy and interaction of the three as distinct parts of a whole helped develop a rich professional identity. I practiced with several groups during those years: in my home agency at the BCW, Division of Foster Home Care when I returned in the summer with foster adolescents and foster and biological parents, in Jewish Family Services with family groups, and in the Colony South Brooklyn Neighborhood House with children, young adults with disabilities and concerned parents of neighborhood school children. I found that while the reciprocal model gave me a plethora of skills and a sense of professional purpose in all settings and groups, 'to mediate the processes through which people and their systems reach out to each another' - parts of each model had virtue for use with varied populations and the models could be blended in actual practice.

Theory building

I was therefore delighted when Papell and Rothman came out with their sequel article in 1980: "Relating the Mainstream Model of Social Work with Groups to Group Psychotherapy and the Structured Group Approach". It was first presented at the First Annual Symposium for the Advancement of Social Work with Groups in Cleveland in 1979. This article represents a dramatic turning point in conceptualization where the authors artfully execute a move above the content to the process of theory making. They move above the discourse of distinct schools of thought (nine approaches were presented in Roberts' and Northen's *Theories of Social Work With Groups* in 1976) and glean common ground for a "mainstream" model of groups. They note that it was Norma Lang (1979) that first coined the phrase "mainstream of social work practice with small groups". One may debate whether there is a mainstream at all, now or then, but that is too abstract. In the trenches, in the realities of practice, a common element "mainstream" model does guide our actions. Whether it is a model or theory that we have learned, or an intuitive response, we do what the moment demands. But we base this, even subconsciously, on knowing of various sorts. For this practitioner and educator the assertion that there is a central identity of social work practice with groups with common elements characterized by "common goals, mutual aid, and non-synthetic experiences" is both anchoring and freeing. Papell and Rothman note that this incorporates the perspective of Gisela Konopka, another of our giants, who insisted on a membership perspective and emphasized that the emotional impact of group association and the action-oriented input of groups are "the two prongs of social work intent"(1978:124). While still valuing the novel, a mainstream model gives us the parameters of what is valued and acceptable practice and what is outside of that. It recognizes that group members are active not passive and that "spontaneous and meaningfully evolving group processes are the instrumental means for realizing group purpose in the mainstream model." It means that we do not manipulate people and that we expect people to "take responsibility to work together toward their own ends (1980: 8, 9)." The group and its members are a living, non static entity. Groups develop as individuals interact even as individuals and societies develop in interaction with one another. The roles of the worker are varied but the stance of the worker is to promote mutual aid and reduce social distance by authenticity and "abrogating the mystique of professionalism" (1980:11).

By contrast, in group psychotherapy an "expert" role of the worker is often built in. Papell and Rothman point out ways in which the skills of social work with groups and group therapy may overlap and enrich each other. They also point out distinct differences and it remains helpful to know the difference between the two. Helen Northen (1969) was also an early synthesizer of clinical social work and normative group work. In her 1995 clinical social work book she contrasts clinical social workers and other helping professionals. She quotes Papell as saying that clinical social workers work to change destructive social forces and develop resources (1995:10). A key difference in group practice is the assumption of the shared authority of the worker and the group in social work with groups. Similarly, while there are many adaptations of the structured group that may enhance social work with groups, the role of the worker as teacher/authority may present some difficulty.

Many claim the mainstream model as underpinning for their own group work theories. Norma Lang (2010) in her recent book *Group Work Practice to Advance Social Competence* bases her practice model "for populations who are not socially competent enough to construct and use groups" on her own "Broad Range Model..."(1972) and the Mainstream Model of Papell and Rothman. She notes that "the mainstream model contains the view of an integral, balanced relationship between the content and process of the group experience....progressing as two movements in process together...." (2010:3). The mainstream model, with its above noted characteristics, was a forerunner of empowerment oriented social work practice and the "empowerment group" approach that I develop in my book (Lee 1994; 2001 and Lee and Hudson, 2011).

In my teaching career of 27 years I worked hard to help students develop a both/and approach rather than an either/or approach to practice. Part of this is a fight against oversimplification and the beginners' need for certainty. I believe that both/and thinking and approaches come with a sense of professional maturity and experience, and with growing tolerance of uncertainty. In *The Empowerment Approach to Social Work Practice: Building the Beloved Community*, (1994; 2001) I blended elements of several approaches into a conceptual framework with the integrated goal of personal, communal and political empowerment. The book remains unique because it questions the dichotomy of the personal and political levels of being as it focuses on building the beloved community. It uses multiple perspectives to weave together clinical, individual, group, communal, political, feminist, and cultural knowledge and skills to build a broad based practice paradigm.

It was in the Fifth Annual AASWG Symposium in 1983 that Ruby Pernell noted that "group work is a natural vehicle for empowerment" and that empowerment practice by its very definition cannot remain politically neutral (1986:111). Hirayama and Hirayama (1986), and Coppola and Rivas (1986), also discussed empowerment at this same Symposium. While I valued Barbara Solomon's seminal book *Black Empowerment* written in 1976, the Fifth Symposium (1983) was my first hearing of the concept of empowerment applied to social work practice with groups and I was hooked. In 1984 at the Sixth Annual Symposium in Chicago I discussed empowerment as central to group work function and illustrated this with my work with homeless women in a large urban shelter (1986).

In 1988 at the Ninth Symposium masterfully chaired by Jim Garland, both Elizabeth Lewis and Margot Breton broke new and exciting ground related to empowerment practice, Lewis in deftly relating feminist perspectives to group work (1992) and Breton in making comparisons of liberation theology and radical social work practice with the poor (1989). Margot Breton presented a paper on "Liberation

Theology, Group Work, and the Right of the Poor and Oppressed to Participate in the Life of the Community" that challenged those elements in our theoretical models that lean toward paternalism and limited empowerment, and emphasized the relinquishing of power by the worker and any paternalistic system. She recounted the courage of the clergy in South America and the development of small group base communities. These communities empowered the poor to speak in their own voices thus "declericalizing" the role of the clergy thereby countering the powerful Roman Catholic Church hierarchy (1989). This re-introduction (for me) of liberation theology now seen in a social work context was to have a far reaching effect on my thinking and being that has gone beyond social work to influencing my second career as a validly ordained 'rebel' Roman Catholic woman priest, a priest of the poor (2008; 2010), who is part of a justice and service-oriented movement where inclusivity and equality among all people prevail. In accepting ordination as a call and an act of conscience we are breaking canon law 1024 that says only men can be ordained. In 1988, Breton was optimistic about the impact of liberation theology on the church, but the backlash was quick and merciless - power does whatever it takes to maintain itself. Like the liberation theologians, we have been battered and marginalized by the church in its effort to maintain the status quo of the all male hierarchy. And like them, we refuse to go away and continue to share "clerical power" and all power with the people. It is the community that has the power. Breton (2011) continues to challenge groups to widen the scope of their vision beyond themselves to enliven their commitment to social justice and actually work toward justice in the world around them. This too is a challenge to the church. I could not have envisioned the impact of Breton's 1988 paper on my theorizing and my very life and its direction. For me, now, the two professions overlap in many ways, particularly in the pursuit of social justice.

In 1991 Ben-Zion Shapiro concluded that the papers noted above (of Elizabeth Lewis, and Margot Breton) along with the work of Gail Goldberg and Ruth Middleman (1989), and Judith Lee (1987) are theoretically "groundbreaking" (1991:16). Rhonda Hudson writes about the Empowerment Model as one of four "major models" in the section on "Group Work Major Models" in the *Encyclopedia of Social Work with Groups,* edited by Alex Gitterman and Bob Salmon (2011). She noted that Lee (1994; 1997; 2001) and Lorraine Gutierrez (with Edith Lewis, 1999) "have led in advances to increase knowledge and understanding of this group approach" (2011:48).

For me, the empowerment group is at the heart of the empowerment approach to social work practice. As noted in the chapter on the empowerment approach by Judith Lee and Rhonda Hudson in Francis Turner's 5th Edition of *Interlocking Theoretical Approaches* (2011: 157-178), "Formed or natural groups can encompass a variety of empowerment purposes. A blending of critical education and conscientization group methods with the interactionist and mainstream models form a foundation for the empowerment group" (165). Thus I am indebted to Papell and Rothman's thinking in the mainstream model of social work with groups as it is a core around which this approach has been developed.

Some practice examples

In thinking about knowledge for group work practice with "new and not new populations" in 1992, Papell suggested that phenomenological knowing goes beyond positivist knowing in that, in interaction the person to be known can and does convey beyond actual content, the essence to be known, that is, who they really are (1992:31-35). Further she thought that for those struggling with alcoholism in families of origin, "the concepts of progression, process development and growth over time, and the dialectical psychological significance of spirituality" in group member's lives were relevant to the processes and skills the group worker uses to "foster the interactional life in groups" (1992:34). With the populations I now serve, the veracity of these words guides me. I have let go of all stereotypes and pigeon-hole definitions about people and listen and search for the essence in each one that includes the unfolding of their lives, their own sense of spirituality and the ways in which they grow in social interaction and empowerment on all levels.

The setting is Good Shepherd Ministries of Southwest Florida, a non-profit agency serving the homeless, formerly homeless, and very low income community residents. I am both Pastor and social worker. The work is demanding and stretches me to use both professions, and secular and spiritual services to the maximum, spontaneously, sometimes interchangeably and as each is needed. The premise we operate on is inclusivity: that all are welcome in whatever we are doing. We serve a full range of people, of all ages, all races and all religions and of no religion. Our community is about two-thirds African-American. In combining those who volunteer and serve with those who receive, and also serve as one group/ "one church", we serve both the poor and the well off. We serve those who struggle with addictions and with mental illness and those who do not but struggle with the inequities of life.

We began with a once-a-week program of feeding homeless and hungry people outdoors in a public park. We offered a hot meal and clothing and social services first and those who wanted to remain also participated in worship with us afterward. At the peak of this program lasting from 2007-2009, up to 150 individuals would attend the meal and 35 or so would remain for worship services. About half of this latter group formed the core group and are with me until this day. I wrote a book about this experience including reflections on the group and its members and a qualitative study about 175 participants' views of God, church and their own needs called *Come By Here: Church with the Poor* (2010). The faith expressed was inspiring.

In a process recording of one evening in the park during a torrential rainstorm I noted: "I was drowned with them tonight and it forged a new level of solidarity - maybe a kind of baptism". I then describe the crowd including Troy, an uninsured jobless laborer, who hobbled toward us in his underwear. He had been discharged from the hospital after treatment for injuries from a hit and run accident. "Soon our elders (the core group who attend worship regularly) brought me to Troy. I got his story as I gave him clothing. I asked some of the elders to 'stick with him'. The elders helped him get into the clothes". They also brought me to Samuel, an epileptic who often has to be lifted out of the ditches on the roadside. We had a new pair of shoes for him and he couldn't get them on. I sat him down, got down on my knees and wrestled his muddy shoes and socks off. I got one on and he got one on. Ben and Rafe offered me their arms and they also stood Sam up. He was so happy he started dancing and we all joined in, right there in the rain. Then the downpour accelerated. About fifty remained to eat the food huddled together under the shelter including one woman in a wheelchair and another with a shopping cart. At one point, I stepped outside and let the rain wash over me. I felt it as God's tears- and I cried tears- of rage and thanksgiving. Rage that this mostly right-wing town has so little for its poorest citizens and thanksgiving at the mutual aid and loving service of one to the other. In the worship service we reflected on loving and serving one another and what made it hard to do that. All of the abhorrent social conditions they endure were named and validated. Ralph, who is over 350 pounds and can hardly walk, was the first man who asked me to pray with him in 2007. He said "just about everything makes it hard, but whatever it is, I try to move it out of the way". We prayed that all basic needs might be met and that we could do something to make it happen together" (Lee, 2010).

By now, I am happy to say, that Ralph and all of the 'elders' and many others who began with us in the park are in permanent affordable housing and have the services and incomes they need to survive. They continue to be instrumental in helping others to gain the same. At this writing we have helped 67 people to attain and, for the most part, sustain housing. Over half of these also have benefits and incomes. We continue to sustain those who do not in a number of ways.

We no longer do the outside feeding program but we serve hot meals on Tuesdays and Sundays and provide social services on Tuesdays. In 2008 we bought a house near the park where we have a transitional living program, Joshua House that has served twenty-one men and two women. The main part of the house is our church that extends into the kitchen. It is our meeting room, our dining room, and our large living room where fellowship and social interaction using a clubhouse and small group model takes place weekly. Picnic tables in the backyard absorb the overflow of people eating and sharing friendship. There are two small rooms to meet with individuals and groups of our children and youth. The core group of elders has grown and helps us to serve old friends and newcomers alike. The space is not large and when we squeeze over fifty inside we realize the need for expansion of our facilities. This is a problem that we are addressing as a group for a move may mean losing families from the neighborhood.

Empowerment is lived. In the Sunday service I have one of the elders, Harry, a devout, formerly homeless African-American man of 60, lead in prayer and in "preaching" after I do in our interactive style homily. He also co-leads with me on Tuesdays. Lanetta, another of our elders also co-leads on Tuesdays. She is a small intelligent white woman in her early fifties who suffered with untreated mental illness causing agitated and aggressive behavior that got her rejected everywhere in town. Now, with treatment and after living in Joshua House for half a year, she is independently housed, and is once again a Mom and Grand-Mom to her family. She and Harry, Ralph and others freely share their stories and wisdom. Whenever we come together, the message is all are equal and your word counts as much as my word. Also, in Sunday worship all present say the words usually reserved for the priest/pastor alone. We celebrate interdependence and live by the Yoruba proverb that says

"I am because we are."

I submit this Tuesday group meeting as an example of mutual aid blending the social and the spiritual, and learning to see the essence of people that we interact with in our helping capacities.

"In a recent Tuesday group about fourteen of our regular people and a few others attended our pre-meal meeting. Lanetta brought everyone grapefruits from her tree. Phyllis brought her small grandchildren and all were moved as they sang along with us. Rafe asked what we are reading today. They love to read and discuss scriptural passages; the pace is fast and lively. I keep this grounded with asking for examples from their lives. The focus was on a passage about forgiving "seventy times seven" and the meaning of forgiveness in their lives. Dewane shared a difficult problem with a man who was trying to run his life. He was trying to work up the courage to say something before he hurt someone. Harry shared how 'holding it in" led to explosive behavior toward family members that took away from who he knew he was. As he learned to share his anger and frustration "in little bits" he found himself forgiving those who upset him most, and free to enjoy those members again. He reflected on some of the kids in his family who were like some of the kids in the church, who worked his "last nerve". As I have asked him to mentor some of the boys, I added that one of them worked my last nerve too and how I "lost it" with him. Ralph talked about the Apostle Paul turning himself around and he thought those kids could turn it around as we have patience. Phyllis said patience was a virtue but not easy to come by. Harry talked about learning from kids and those who frustrate us most. Dewane thanked Harry for guiding him and shared his intentions to speak up so he could then forgive. Lanetta then said that she had found forgiveness with us. "You know, I had a lot of problems and no one wanted me around. No one forgave me even when I changed. The police didn't forgive me. I still can't go into the park after two years of being well. The food agency doesn't forgive me, I can't go there. Even the uptown church doesn't let me in so they can't see the new person that I am. But my family has forgiven and here I know that I am forgiven and loved for who I am. Most of all, here I learned to forgive myself and to become a forgiving person. I am always so happy to be here with everyone." I reached over and put my arm around her and Harry said that's right and true for all of us. And, he added, "I, for one, couldn't believe that you could change, but I am a witness - you did". He began applauding her with all joining in".

We serve about twenty children and youth ranging in age from three to eighteen. We meet every Sunday and also do summer camp and trips and reward good grades. Only in the last year have I been able to find the space to separate the older and younger kids. The combined age group broke all the group work 'rules' -it was overly heterogeneous, overly large and not racially or gender balanced. Two of the teenagers have profound emotional problems with different degrees of selective mutism. One of the younger boys is on heavy psychiatric medication and another is slow. What are the chances of that working out in a "non-therapeutic" group? Or was it that? It was a class-group that also combined talking, teaching, activities, and the sharing of feelings and experiences. It was at once structured and unstructured. And yet it worked. And it continued to work when a brilliant African-American High School Senior was able to co-lead with me and allow me to do only part of the class. She was initially sorely tested by the older boys. I mediated and soon she became a wonderful role model and they worked well together until she left for college. The content and the process became one as the feelings of belonging and helping and caring for one another developed.

The teenagers give me quite a challenge. There are six regulars in the current teen class ranging from 14-18. They are evenly divided by gender with only one white member, an older girl who barely whispers. An older boy also has problems speaking and the others never stop talking. Who would choose this composition - and yet it too works. If I can hang in there, their slow but near miraculous gains will continue. As for phases or stages of group development, Garland, Jones and Kolodny's classic typology developed with youth (1973) still helps me understand the movement in the group from approach-avoidance to power and control, intimacy, differentiation/ work and separation. As a group, they are well into the work stage. But each one is at a different place with it. No matter what, I convey my love to the group as a whole, and to each one, every week. And they reciprocate -but power and control is never dead with teenagers.

Malekoff (2009) says it perfectly: he notes that credentials don't impress kids, not even the Roman collar when I wear it or my doctorates when they discovered them. There is a need to be flexible, to check your ego at the door, to have a sense of humor and to lose one's self importance. The latter he sees as a gateway to effective group practice with teens. Wow! What good learning for a priest that is a social worker who is nowhere near a saint and on the verge of being over the hill!

It is not easy - but it is worth it. In every class meeting there is a challenge to balance content and process and to weave their experiences in with the content. Some like nothing better than to get me to drop the content completely, while others prefer it and feign sleep when we talk about difficult life experiences like the extreme degree of violence they witness. While some of the girls are working with energy, one never smiled, one boy is a joker and another constantly farts in class making us all leave unless I send him out first. They constantly up date my understandings of their slang and are sometimes gleeful when I really miss something. But here is the joy: now they laugh, smile, learn, and grow in individual ways and as a group. For each one school grades have improved. Ty, 18, who did not speak for the entire first year, is now chatty, funny, argumentative, angry and annoying (a lot closer to normal)! Sometimes I have to silence him to move us along and he is obstinate and not at all respectful. Last week he complained that I didn't listen to him. I listened and said that he was sometimes right about that. He was stunned. Then I made an agreement with him so I could get on to the content. Our brightest girl, Tasha, told him that he didn't listen to anyone so he needed to learn that too. Strike one for mutual aid! With Marie, who didn't respond or read when asked, it was the group that helped me to demand some work from her. Each week she would forget her glasses. I asked her to wear them and nothing happened. Finally the group members told her that it was time to wear them and to participate. She returned with her glasses and began to read and answer softly. Two of the others sincerely commended her for this and it was a new ballgame after that.

So what I have learned in my later years of practice is that nothing has to be or can be "by the book" – it is really, as Papell said (1992), by the "essence" of the group members and ourselves interacting with them that groups work. And they work better than anything we know.

Knowledge and thinking
about social work with groups

In 1982 Dr. Papell presented a significant paper at the closing Plenary Session of the Fourth Annual AASWG Symposium in Toronto, Canada. In "Group Work in the Profession of Social Work: Identity in Context" (1982) she discussed the reciprocal relation of group work and the social work profession. Using Homans' concept that the behavior of the group is determined by the environment and in turn changes that environment she explores the interchange between the two. She asks a question that is as important now as it was then: how do we influence the profession of social work, and how in turn are we influenced by it? (1982:1195). She notes that the profession has gone through periods of "searching for its wholeness" of distilling common ground and joining what were once separate methods under one roof. While group work became part of NASW in 1955, group work had a distinct history separate from social work. She resonates with Gisela Konopka's view that "despite being taught early at a school of social work, its integration into the profession was not an easy one" (1983:6). However, Katy suggests that the profession itself could not realize its social mission, social change challenge, and psycho-social domain without group work. She saw group work's place in the profession as a complex unity, a "dialectical unity of polarities" (1982:1200). She noted that both systems theory and the integration of the ecological perspective are comfortable territory for group workers as is group action for social change and knowledge of primary groups.

In another place Papell and Rothman highlighted the theoretical contributions of William Schwartz, as a "giant" whose "debate and collaboration with the leadership of the profession advanced the stature and knowledge of the group methodology". They described him as a "savant before his time" with a "sophisticated and imaginative understanding" of systemic interdependence and the strengths of people and the need for operationalized principles to guide the worker's actions that "spurred the theoretical development of methodology and technique"(1986:1-2). They noted that he gave mutual aid a preeminent place in the profession through giving it "a primacy which brought direction and focus to social group work practice..." (1986:1).

In a paper published in 1991 (pp.54-58) Papell and Rothman proposed an impressionistic continuum going from " introspective, existential and process oriented theories to empirical and extraspective theories" by group work thinkers as a "cognitive map for grasping the holistic structure of the field of group work theory". While places on the continuum could be debated, and the list was not exhaustive, thirty-nine group work theorists were placed on the continuum thus describing a rich intellectual environment for the continuation of theory development. In the same paper they made specific proposals for how group work could be included in integrated practice curriculum and field education so that it could remain a vital part of the profession.

In 1982, Papell acknowledges the landmark work of Carel Germain and Alex Gitterman in creating a life model of practice within an ecological perspective (first published in 1980) that kept group work central to the practice approach, but, she wonders why more with group work background are not developing a theory base. She sees group workers as the "bearers of multiplicity in human social experience" and challenges us to think and write less descriptively and more theoretically using this historical knowledge base (1982:1207). I agree with Papell and note that it is the theoretical work of William Schwartz, and of Carel Germain and Alex Gitterman (1980), Ruby Pernell (1986) and Margot Breton (1989), Goldberg and Middleman (1989) and Papell and Rothman themselves who have influenced my own work in theory and practice. I echo Papell's challenge to think and write more theoretically.

It is the role of a senior statesperson in the profession to reflect on what we know and ways of knowing, or the epistemology of the profession as well as its growing body of knowledge and practice wisdom. Dr. Papell does this in her 1992 and 1997 articles in *Social Work with Groups*.

In 1992 she reflected on the demands on group workers to know enough to serve a wide variety of populations, old and new to group work. She noted the ease of information access on various populations and their particular needs. Yet, perhaps most importantly in the midst of the information explosion she suggested that "We begin with people in their life space and learn the specialness of their life situations as we engage with them" (1992:24). This shares knowledge for practice with our group members who are also our teachers. She quotes George Getzel, another profoundly scholarly practitioner and educator, who noted: "it is not through a positivist epistemology and rationality that much of social work with groups is done. The complexity (of people and workers in groups) precludes a deterministic stance. We group workers instantly experience the emergent every time we enter the exhilarating chaos of group life" (1985). Papell discussed a more phenomenological approach to knowing people and the emerging, in vivo, aspect of the human condition. This thinking of Papell and Getzel is ahead of its time and more properly fits in the post modern era where all knowledge can be questioned and deconstructed, and the emergent is hoped for and welcomed. Papell went on to discuss the world view of social group work and its filtration through the individual worker. She also joined Middleman and Goldberg (1985) in valuing uncertainty in order to move empathically into the world of the group and in appreciating other ways of knowing through intuition, creativity and practice wisdom. Papell noted that in such a world view values and ethics are "grounded in love of the human conditions, individual, group and community" (and interdependence) (1992:28, 29). While not devaluing empirical knowledge, or the need for accountability, she challenges the profession to consider other approaches to knowing about people and their groups that can enliven practice and professional knowledge. She also noted that understandings of a person's spirituality is important in understanding a practice population which she knew well, adult children of alcoholics. In 1997, she again discussed the impact of working in the Alcoholism Clinic on her viewpoint that workers need to understand the meaning of spirituality and religion, organized or not, in their group members' lives (p. 15). All of the above noted concepts are useful to me in my current work with groups, and in my bridge making efforts between the professions of social work and ministry. It is finding that which enlivens people and draws them together to help one another and challenge injustice that is the essence of both for me.

In 1997, Papell looked back on theory development and practice since the exciting and fertile era that produced her thinking on separate models, and later on the mainstream model. She also recalled the First Annual Symposium and its "wonderful spirit of inclusion, validation and humanity that is imbedded in group work ideology (that) was compelling and inspiring" (1997:10). I would stop for a moment here and say that here the person and the thought expressed are indeed one. I could say that Katy is the spirit of group work personified for her wonderful spirit of inclusion, validation and humanity is compelling and inspiring today as ever to a profession that needs its humanity now more than ever before.

Papell went on to note that today's social workers often know a great deal about the problems their clients are facing, for example, alcoholism, Alzheimer's disease, cancer, various illnesses, etc. and "very little about group process and helping the group to grow". She discussed a seminar she held with a group of alcoholism counselors where Ruth Middleman's first practice principle "Think Group!"(Middleman & Goldberg, 1985) and such concepts as conflict resolution, problem solving, scapegoating and stages of group development opened a whole new line of exploration for them. She concluded that the time honored group work maxim applies: "Attention to both process and content is vital. We must be specialists on two counts!"(1997:13). She suggested that group work theory now must include "knowledge that is rooted in the problem and in the interactional aspects of the problem" (13).

Here are the challenges proposed to us by Dr. Papell: that social workers who work with groups continue to develop theory out of our knowledge base and practice experiences with groups; that we value and utilize all ways of knowing and move beyond overvaluing positivistic thinking; that we seek out 'essence' in our group members and our group interactions; that we see people as whole beings in community with psychosocial and spiritual dimensions; remain guided by our values regarding people and groups and not primarily by the need for accountability measures; and that we develop knowledge rooted in problems people face and in the interactional aspects of the problem including how group work knowledge and skills can help guide our practice.

Further, we are challenged to grow in wisdom, grace, elegance and the pursuit of justice under the influence of our very special founder and foremother, Dr. Catherine P. Papell, our collective ego-ideal and our quintessential group worker. Katy, you do transform the world!

You Transform The World
For Dr. Catherine P. Papell

Katy,
You are our Jane Addams
blending cause and function,
democracy and full participation,
settlement and justice,
beauty, music and art,
learning and a fair start,
bread and peace in time of war,
our ambassador abroad
and inspiring activist
for Afghan women and inclusion,
always inclusion for all people

so that the over accumulation
at one end may be shared.
You model still passion and
compassion for people and
for process equal to outcomes-
servant, savant, sage,
and yet, you know no age.

You are our Bertha C. Reynolds,
blending method and action
never bending to the popular
or the easy, your heart is
with the working people always.
Your work with those addicted
and their families, and with
the homeless and outcast
continuing into time when
others would have simply rested.

Complex thinker, questioning,
challenging-creating higher ground
for our thinking-but your doing
is the harder and better part....
You are our loving woman,
our ever curious intellectual
with a conscience and a
heart of pure-spun gold.
You are our synthesizer and integrator
so that the theories fit like puzzle pieces
and group work is one.
You are our bright star,
our ethicist, keeping our
moral compass pointed north
anchoring us to our groupwork values.
You call us to love beyond our powers,
to give, to think,
to challenge the way things are
and by our actions usher in
the way things are supposed to be....

Thank you for the example

of lifelong dedication to the work
with energy, love and caring.
Thank you for keeping on,
for teaching us, and reaching us
with who you are
and who we can be-
as social workers-
as those who serve one another-
dedicated to groups that form
and connect us to the end.
And most of all,
it is the greatest pleasure
to call you friend,
and ask you to accept the
gratitude we here extend
and our unending love.
Rev. Dr. Judy Lee- Excerpted from Poem for AASWG Honoring at Hull
House, 2009

References

Bennett, L. (1978). Group service for COPD out-patients: Surmounting the obstacles. *Social Work with Groups*, 2 (2), 145-160.

Berman-Rossi, T., Ed. (1994). *Social Work: The Collected Writings of William Schwartz*. Itasca,Ill. F.E. Peacock Publishers, Inc.

Breton, M. (1989). Liberation theology, group work, and the right of the poor and oppressed to participate in the life of the community. *Social Work with Groups*, 12 (3), 5-18.

Breton, M. (2011). Citizenship consciousness, nonbounded solidarity, and social justice. *Social Work with Groups*, 34 (1), 35-50. Doi:10.1080/0160 9513.2010.520103

Coppola, M. & Rivas, R. (1986). The task-action group technique: A case study in empowering the elderly. In M. Parnes (Ed.),*Innovations in Social Group Work: Feedback from Practice to Theory* (pp.133-148). New York: Haworth Press.

Garland, J. A., Jones, H.E., & Kolodny, R. L. (1973). A model for stages of development in social work groups. In S. Bernstein (Ed.), *Explorations in Group Work* (pp. 17-71). Boston , Mass: Milford House, Inc.

Germain, C. B. & Gitterman, A. (1980). *The Life Model of Social Work Practice.* New York: Columbia University Press.

Getzel, G. S. (1985). Teaching group work skill through reflection in action. Paper presented at VII Annual Symposium on social Work with Groups, Rutgers University, 1985.

Gitterman, A. & Shulman, L. (1986). *Mutual Aid Groups and the Life Cycle.* Itasca, Ill: F.E. Peacock, Publishers.

Gitterman, A. & Shulman L. (2005). *Mutual Aid Groups, Vulnerable & Resilient Populations, and the Life Cycle.* New York: Columbia University Press.

Gitterman, A. & Salmon, R. (Eds.) (2009). *Encyclopedia of Social Work with Groups.* New York: Routledge.

Goldberg, G. W. & Middleman, R.R. (1989). *The Structural Approach to Direct Practice in Social Work.* New York: Columbia University Press.

Gutierrez, L.M. & Lewis, E.A. (1999). *Empowering Women of Color.* New York: Columbia University Press.

Hirayama, H. & Hirayama, K. (1986). Empowerment through group participation: Process and goal. In M.Parnes (Ed.) *Innovations in Social Group Work: Feedback from Practice to Theory* (pp.119-181). New York: Haworth Press.

Hudson, R.E. (2009). Empowerment model. In A. Gitterman & R. Salmon (Eds.) *Encyclopedia of Social Work with Groups* (pp.47-50). New York: Routledge.

Konopka, G. (1978). The significance of social group work based on ethical values. *Social Work with Groups,* 1 (2), 123-131.

Konopka, G. (1983). *Social Group Work: A Helping Process 3rd. Edition.* Englewood Cliffs, N.J.: Prentice-Hall, Inc.

Lang, N.C. (1972). A broad range model of practice in the social work group. *Social Service Review* 46 (1), 76—89.

Lang, N.C. (2010). *Group Work Practice to Advance Social Competence.* New York: Columbia University Press.

Lee, J. A. B. (1979). The foster parents' workshop: A social work approach to learning for new foster parents. *Social Work with Groups,* 2 (2), 129-144.

Lee, J. A. B. (1980). *Teaching Behaviors for Perceived Relevance.* DSW Dissertation, Wurzweiler School of Social Work, Yeshiva University, June, 1980.

Lee, J. A. B. (1990). From West Hartford-tribute for Beulah Rothman. *Social Work With Groups,* 13 (4) xiii-xiv.

Lee, J. A. B. (1994). *The Empowerment Approach to Social Work Practice.* New York: Columbia University Press.

Lee, J. A. B. (1997). The empowerment group: The heart of the Empowerment Approach and an antidote to injustice. In J.K. Parry (Ed.), *From Prevention to Wellness through Group Work* (pp. 15-29). New York: Haworth Press.

Lee, J. A. B. (2001). *The Empowerment Approach to Social Work Practice: Building the Beloved Community.* New York: Columbia University Press.

Lee, J. A. B. (2008). A priest of the poor. In McGrath, E.H., Meehan,B.M.,& Raming, I.(Eds). *Women Find A Way: The Movement and Stories of Roman Catholic Women Priests* (pp.77-85). College Station, Texas: Virtualbookworm.com, Publishing, Inc .

Lee, J. A. B. (2010). *Come By Here: Church with the Poor.* Baltimore, Md. : Publishamerica.com.

Lee, J. A. B. & Hudson, R.E. (2011). Empowerment approach to social work practice. In F.J. Turner, *Social Work Treatment: Interlocking Theoretical Approaches,* 5th Ed. (pp.157- 178). New York: Oxford University Press, Inc.

Lewis, E. Regaining promise: Feminist perspectives for social group work practice. In J.A. Garland (Ed.) *Group Work Reaching Out: People, Places and Power* (pp. 271-284). New York: Haworth Press, Inc.

Malekoff, A. (2009). Gatekeepers, gatecrashers, and gateways in group work with kids: A mystery story. *Social Work with Groups,* 32 (3),193-208.Doi: 10.1080/01609510802527425

Middleman, R.R. (1978). Returning group process to group work. *Social Work with Groups,* 1 (1): 15-26.

Middleman, R.R. & Goldberg, G.W. (1985). Maybe it's a priest or a lady with a hat with a tree on it, or is it a bumble bee? Teaching group workers to see. *Social Work with Groups,*8 (1),3- 15.

Northen, H. (1969). *Social Work with Groups.* New York: Columbia University Press.

Northen, H. (1995).*Clinical Social Work: Knowledge and Skills.* New York: Columbia Univ. Press.

Papell, C. P. (1978). *A Study of Styles of Learning for Direct Social Work Practice.* DSW Dissertation, Wurzweiler School of Social Work, Yeshiva University, June, 1978.

Papell, C. P. (1982). Group work in the profession of social work: Identity in context (pp. 1193- 1209). In Lang, N.C. & Marshall, C. (Eds.). *Patterns in the Mosaic.* Proceedings of the 1982 Fourth AASWG Symposium, Ontario, Canada: University of Toronto Press.

Papell, C. P. (1990). In Memoriam-Beulah Rothman. *Social Work with Groups,* 13(3) vii-ix.

Papell, C. P. (1992). Group work with new populations: Knowledge and knowing. In Garland, J.A. (Ed). *Group Work Reaching Out: People, Places and Power* (pp. 23-36). New York: the Haworth Press.

Papell, C. P. (1997). Thinking about thinking about group work: Thirty years later. *Social Work with Groups* 20 (4) 5-18.

Papell, C. P. and Rothman, B. (1966). Social Group work models: Possession and heritage. *Journal of Education for Social Work*, 2 (2)66-77.

Papell, C. P. & Rothman,B. (1980). Relating the mainstream model of social work with groups to group psychotherapy and the structured group approach. *Social Work with Groups*, 3(2), 5-23.

Papell, C. P. & Rothman,B. (1991). Issues for education for social work with groups. In Weil, M. Chau, K. & Southerland D. (Eds.) *Theory and Practice in Social Group Work: Creative Connections* (pp.53-69). New York: The Haworth Press.

Pernell, R. B. (1986). Empowerment and social group work. In M. Parnes (Ed.) *Innovations in Social Group Work: Feedback from Practice to Theory* (pp. 107-118). New York: Haworth Press.

Ramey, J. (2009). AASWG. In A. Gitterman and R. Salmon, (Eds). *Encyclopedia of Social Work with Groups*, (pp.19-24). New York: Routledge.

Roberts, R. W. & Northen, H. (1976). *Theories of Social Work with Groups* .New York: Columbia.

Schwartz, W. (1961). The social worker in the group. In T. Berman-Rossi (Ed.) Social Work: The Collected Writings of William Schwartz (pp. 257-276). Itasca, Illinois: F.E. Peacock Publishers.

Schwartz, W. (1964). The Classroom Teaching of Social Work with Groups: Some Central Problems. In T. Berman-Rossi, (Ed) *Social Work : The Collected Writings of William Schwartz* (pp. 574-582). Itasca, Illinois: F.E.Peacock Publishers.

Schwartz, W. (1971). On the use of groups in social work practice. In W. Schwartz and S. Zalba (Eds.) *The Practice of Group Work* (3-24). New York: Columbia University Press.

Shapiro, B-Z. (1991). Social action, the group, and society. *Social Work with Groups*,14 (3-4),7- 22.

Shulman, L. (1972). *Group Work Skill and Effective College Instruction*. Ed.D Dissertation, Temple University.

Shulman, L. (1992). *The Skills of Helping: Individuals, Families, and Groups*, 3rd Edition. Itasca, Illinois, F.E. Peacock Publishers.

Shulman, L. (2011). *Dynamics and Skills of Group Counseling*. Belmont, CA: Brooks-Cole.

Solomon, B. B. (1976). *Black Empowerment: Social Work in Oppressed Communities*. New York, Columbia University Press.

6
Walking the talk: Utilizing groupwork in gatekeeping social work education

Mary Wilson

Introduction

This chapter explores using groupwork as a gatekeeping mechanism. It will consider the challenges that arise in maintaining professional standards while actualising principles of access and social inclusion in social work education and training for non-traditional students. Professional behaviour formation is at the core of programmes which seek to educate the professional. This task may be enhanced or impeded by many issues including the students' previous life and work experiences, professional accreditation criteria, field work agency values, and institutional norms and parameters regarding access and participation. Gatekeeping is a core process in the delivery of professional social work education.

The chapter will explore gatekeeping as social inclusion, a core value in programmes seeking to construct the professional identity of a non-traditional student. Then, a review of screening out or inclusion that is required when students are found to be unsuitable for professional practice will be undertaken. The use of the groupwork modality to support tutors, practitioners and service users in student selection and progression will be considered for its relevance in achieving successful outcomes in both spheres. The BASS (Bachelor of Applied Social Studies), an exit route programme devised for students who are deemed unsuitable for professional training at University College Cork Ireland, will be used to provide an example of resolving the gatekeeping debate in practice.

Background

Principles of human rights and social justice are fundamental to social work. These values are central to defining who we are as a profession, why we do what we do and how we do it! "Human rights and social justice serve as the motivation and justification for social work action. In solidarity with those who are disadvantaged, the profession strives to alleviate poverty and to liberate vulnerable and oppressed people in order to promote social inclusion" (NSWQB 2003). Education is a major strategy for fostering social inclusion. Thus, issues of access and widening participation are fundamental to the ethos of professional training programmes for the non-traditional student cohort. This approach emphasises commitment and willingness to walk the tight rope between oppressed/marginalised people and the social and political structures that have contributed to their exclusion (Friere, 1973; Lee, 1994; Lordan & Wilson, 2002; Parker, 2007). In practice, social inclusion involves actualising the values of equality, recognition and participation. As a social work educator, I believe that groupwork is the modality best suited to managing the tension inherent in that polarity and for modelling reflective functioning for best practice.

Gatekeeping is central to the process of professional formation. The term *gatekeeping* evokes different responses among those who are responsible for the evaluation, selection and retention of students. One view encompasses a process where students are nurtured through the educational enterprise to ensure that they successfully complete the course and are competent to practise when they graduate. Another is to see it as a way of selectively shutting the gate at some point in the student's journey when s/he is found to be unsuitable for practice in the field of social work. Gatekeeping issues can be present when the student applies to the programme or manifest at a later stage. Unsuitability for practice can occur for any number of reasons, such as difficulty with integrating theory into practice, the wounded-impaired helper phenomenon, extreme egotism or inappropriate behaviour (Gibbs & Macy, 2000; Lafrance, Gray, & Herbert 2004). Regardless, the script for the gatekeeping process cannot be written specifically, as one size does not always fit all. Differences in programme content, institutional contexts and the student cohort will be influential in determining the kinds of responses that will 'fit'. In the following pages the issues that have arisen at the University College Cork Ireland will be reviewed, and some specific gatekeeping responses explored.

Gatekeeping at the entry level stage

Consideration of licensing and application processes within global and local contexts

The introduction of the Byelaw in May 2011, the first statutory instrument of its kind under the Health and Social Care Professionals Act, 2005, completes the process by which the profession of social work in Ireland will be regulated in the 21st century. The right to apply for registration which had previously been issued by the University on completion of either a BSW or MSW degree will now be issued via application for registration to CORU (Health and Social Care Professionals Council, Dublin, Ireland), the new regulatory authority. CORU is also responsible for the licensing of continuing professional development initiatives, course accreditation and fitness to practice. These changes bring Ireland into line with the USA, UK and some jurisdictions in the EU, where the licensing power rests outside of the remit of the university.

At the local level, University College Cork offers two professional social work education programmes, an MSW and a BSW. Both courses integrate university based and agency based learning to provide the requisite academic and professional knowledge, skills and values for professional practice. Graduates from both courses gain the same license to practice in the profession on completion of their programme. The BSW course is unique in its focus on the mature/non-traditional student cohort and its mission to combat social exclusion.

Students wishing to come on the BSW course make application

through the Central Admissions Office (CAO). This is a twofold process involving an aptitude test as a pre-selection mechanism and an interview. The course team, practitioners and service users make up the panel of interviewers who make the final selection of the 25 students who will gain entry to Year one. The average age of students who apply is mid to late thirties. While a gender imbalance exists, with more women than men represented in the student cohort, there is also greater evidence of multiculturalism from increasing participation by students from Africa and Eastern Europe. In the main, the students are typically those who are returning to full time education for a 'second chance' or those who seek retraining from another career. They are assertive, highly articulate and most are cognisant of the privilege of being at university. The exit route programme, the Bachelor of Applied Social Studies (BASS) was inaugurated in 2008, and runs concurrently with the BSW in years three and four. Currently three students have been offered and/or are completing the BASS.

Consideration of previous life and work experience

For activate inclusion in the educational sphere we must create an environment within which people can develop to their fullest potential. Students come to the social work course with a wealth of prior knowledge and life experience. This previous life and work experience serves as a rich resource for learners and teachers alike. Within contemporary social work education there has been much discussion on the use and relevance of principles of adult education (Foley, 2004; Sankaran, 2001; Bamber, 1995). One of main issues facing us as educators is to create an educational environment in which the previous life and work experiences of students can be validated and used in the teaching process as well as examined for its applicability and transfer to the arena of professional practice. In this context, the support for the learning endeavour becomes central. We employ a number of group based educational methods which are designed to support the formation of the professional in training.

Gatekeeping during the educational process

Initially when a group of students embark on a course there will be different needs, styles of learning, levels of motivation and/or resistance to the learning endeavour. In terms of professional formation, balancing participants' needs with the requirements of the university will pose a challenge to the creativity of any programme team. Non-traditional students generally have high support needs for the different stages of the learning process. Many students begin by identifying and articulating the discontinuities between previous work contexts where the emphasis is on task, productivity and an external locus of control with the university's emphasis on theory, applied knowledge and professionalism. The idea of professional formation is one that needs to be acknowledged and integrated in the new learning context, and must be constructed collaboratively with students.

A triad of approaches using groupwork principles

Small tutorial groups are formed at the outset of programme and facilitated by course tutors to build the learning community. Three models/approaches using groupwork principles are central to the success of this collaboration:

1. Models of adult education, which foster equality and participation by students in the learning process, are used. The knowledge building process is one that students struggle with continually and sometimes resist. There are a number of stages in this process. Initially many students come as consumers of the service of education and articulate themselves as service users. The next stage concerns the engagement and use of self in the learning process; and later the students come to understand their responsibility towards the other: the service user, who is the invisible presence in all our relationships as tutors and practice teachers, and is the *end user* of this process of education and training. Collaborative small group and active learning approaches are particularly useful

in addressing the learning needs of the non-traditional student group while developing and enhancing their sense of professional identity (Smith, 2009). Participation in small learning groups focuses on developing the reflective functioning skills upon which practitioner frames of reference are constructed. Tutors model professional engagement and facilitate its articulation and application to other spheres of work. For example, the social work service user may be reframed as an adult learner using this paradigm, indicating its transferability and applicability to the practice context where it can be used to facilitate service users who are also 'experts by experience' (Preston-Shoot, 2007), to collaborate in the construction of meaning associated with their experiences and to take action based upon it.

2. Enquiry based learning (EBL) utilises and builds on students' prior ways of doing and knowing. EBL is a particularly useful tool for addressing the theory practice dissonance that non-traditional students struggle with and frequently articulate. EBL describes an environment in which the learning is driven by a process of enquiry owned by the student (Kolb, 1984). Using small groups, the teaching focus emphasises student centered learning, experiential learning, and collaborative work which can help to actualise the value of social inclusion in the teaching and learning context. Small groupwork, facilitated by tutors, enables students to identify their own issues and questions, which actualises the purpose of the group. Knowledge gained through this process is more readily retained because it has been acquired by experience and in relation to a real issue/problem.

3. Creative means of working, which support alternative discourses in teaching and learning, are utilized. The discourse of social inclusion has become marginal to the world view that social work is promulgating. It would appear that engaging in the provision of 'packages' of care in the field, and profitable 'packages' of education, are indicators of what is now increasingly valued and affirmed. A Canadian study (Lafrance et al, 2004) suggests that social workers have become overly aligned with the work system that employs them, creating an over-identification with bureaucratic systems instead of the profession or clients served. Social workers' responses to meeting needs with ever declining resources risk neglecting and ignoring the reality of peoples' existence and their struggles. Managerialism has become the dominant discourse in agencies to the exclusion of dialogue and bridge building between

social workers and service users. As educators, we need to contest this world view by offering more creative and intuitive forms of engagement that seek to work in partnership with students and service users in challenging the oppression or injustice of expert systems. Conceptually, social exchange theory and groupwork theory cohere in the strengths perspectives (Saleeby, 2002), thus enabling robust and creative responses to the brief/problem/solving/outcomes driven models currently dominating professional practice. As an educator I believe in parity of esteem for educational initiatives that value cognitive, affective and intuitive processes. My own experiences as an educator have led me to groupwork and maskmaking, (Lordan, Wilson & Quirke, 2007; 2009). These tools support creativity and reflexivity in addressing the post-modern dilemmas of uncertainty, chaos and crisis that are everyday events in the lives of social workers and service users. Social workers in training also learn to acknowledge the equality of cognitive and intuitive processes and endeavour to integrate them in an inclusive pedagogy which supports a diversity of approaches in education and training and produces critically reflective professionals (Wilson & Quirke, 2009).

Groupwork gatekeeping strategies: Group panels and group forums

The role of service users as contributors to the gatekeeping evaluation process

Service users have a vast practice wisdom, which has not as yet been recognised as contributing to the dominant discourse. Its meaningful inclusion in the educational domain requires greater attention in institutional responses to professional education and training. The BSW programme has inaugurated a group panel of service users to assist in the student selection process. The composition includes those who have engaged with child protection and welfare; adoption; disability and the mental health services. For selection in 2012 new members include young people formerly in residential care now living independently. The Selection Co-ordinator conducts a single session training group with the Panel to clarify roles, offer support and ensure that materials are relevant. The service user Panel has been providing this service for four years. Each year it is evident that the group has grown in personal confidence and capacity which is a welcome but secondary outcome of their involvement. Their principal contribution lies in the richness of the wisdom that they bring to the interviewing process. A caveat exists currently, service users do not receive direct payment for their time or expertise. Travel expenses, book vouchers and lunch are offered. Perhaps the next challenge for the activation of social inclusion will be to payment of 'real' money to service users for their services. This is an issue that the course teams are reviewing urgently and creatively as resource allocation becomes more contested.

Service user involvement is a continuous resource for student learning. Current BSW students on fieldwork placement are expected to engage with users in evaluating the quality (or otherwise!) of the service they have delivered. This conversation with service users (Elliott et al 2005) seeks to establish an alternative discourse based on service user need rather than service delivery, and recognition of the service user as a co-equal end user of the professional formation experience. Providing increased opportunities for more meaningful engagement by service users in course delivery and assessment continues to be an evolving objective.

Support for staff serving as gatekeepers

Responding to high support needs of mature students however has its own 'hidden curriculum', which is the need to 'model' good practice in the educational arena. Specifically, for those who are delivering professional education and training it can mean the erosion of self and the lack of institutional recognition of the impact made by the welfare/support component in the teaching, tutoring and academic progression spheres. To contextualise, to date the BSW programme has necessitated attendance at pre-death rites and funerals of three students, attended the 'afters' of a couple of weddings, arranged maternity leave for others, encountered those who have experienced incidents of sexual abuse, domestic violence, mental illness, child and parental hospitalisation, dealt with police clearances that were not clear and interviewed/confronted students who tried intimidation inside and outside of class because of failure to progress. In addition there is a support role to colleagues and other students who have been affected by these experiences. Responding to these challenges, lead to the establishment of a group Tutor's Forum. This remit of this small group was to support team members, clarify and find solutions to the complex issues that professional formation raises for students. The facilitator of the Forum was a practitioner whose long experience in fieldwork supervision has been extremely useful in addressing and resolving the issues that have emerged. As a group, the Forum brought 'the outside in' and takes 'the inside out'. As groupworkers we well know the importance of challenging the isolation that can accompany course delivery with non-traditional students.

Practice Advisory Panels as contributors to the gatekeeping evaluation process

The Tutor's Forum has evolved from the BSW to encompass the wider arena of professional programmes within the School. This segue has been formalised into group Practice Advisory Panels whose membership consists of 6 or so experienced practitioners from a wide variety of contexts. The Practice Advisory Panel meets twice yearly to review the written work undertaken by students from fieldwork as quality control and professional oversight mechanisms. Members of the Panel also offer professional support to Fieldwork personnel and are available to act as mediators in the event of disputes arising from failed practice assessments.

Considerations when screening out unsuitable students

Duty of care

Unsuitability for practice can occur for any number of reasons, including difficulty with incorporating theory into practice, the wounded helper phenomenon, extreme narcissism, or behaviours related to the inability to function within the parameters of professional expectation (Gibbs

& Macy, 2003; Lafrance et al., 2004). As social work educators we have a duty of care to service users who are the end users of all our interventions. We and our colleagues in practice are all gate keepers of professional standards. In light of these issues, there is increasing agreement that screening out social work students whose difficulties are non-academic is a major challenge for educators and consequently for the profession as a whole. Yet given the reality that not all students will meet the necessary professional standards, and in order to protect service users, it is crucial that social work programmes 'do not avoid the difficult issue of failing inadequate students' (Cowburn et al, 2000). Some of the issues that have emerged in actualising the principle of duty of care include:

Promoting diversity

A key principle of social work education concerns the elimination of institutional barriers that impact negatively on dis-advantaged and oppressed groups. Reconciling the need to eliminate discriminatory practices against minorities with the commitment to gatekeeping in professional social work education is an ongoing challenge that frequently leaves staff uncertain and often afraid. In relation to ethnic minorities, does affirmative action mean lowering standards to ensure entry and automatic progression to professional qualification? Does this become discriminatory of non minorities who fail to meet and maintain programme standards? Posing this question serves to highlight how gatekeeping is a particularly sensitive area for teachers and students alike. In my experience, the ability to write clearly and comprehensively in the language of the society within which license to practice will be granted must be a requirement. Indeed report writing and record keeping are core proficiencies in professional social work education, not least for their impact on the lives of service users. In keeping with principles of access and inclusion, support mechanisms are provided and literacy support is offered for dealing with writing and literacy issues. However in a minority of cases this is insufficient to meet the need and leads to inevitable failure on fieldwork placement. Colleagues in the field are understandably perplexed that students seem to pass academic assignments in the first two years of the course while failing report writing while on fieldwork placement in years three and four. Agreed standards of literacy are developed in partnership with accreditation bodies, educators and practitioners requiring on-going dialogue and clarification. From 2012 passing grades on the BSW have been increased from 40% to 50% . This provision will need on-going review and re-evaluation for its effectiveness in raising and maintaining standards of professional training.

Student rights

Ensuring that students' rights are honoured is an ever present challenge in the gatekeeping process. Student's rights are a valued principle that underpins all our work, but are sometimes misinterpreted or misused as with disability legislation. In this context, access to a degree is often seen as an entitlement rather than an opportunity. However carte blanche entitlement to a degree that gives a professional license to practice in the social professions is fraught with dangers that frequently go unrecognised and/or are minimised. In the absence of universal policies and practices that support the screening out of unsuitable or impaired students, we strive to balance the competing needs and rights of both students and service users in the hope that we get the balance right!

Impaired helpers, wounded healers

Impairment in professionals resulting from addiction to substances or behaviours that legitimate abuse; mental illness or emotional (dis)stress is becoming a more visible issue in students applying for professional programmes. Social work students report a greater incidence of psychosocial trauma and dysfunctional families than students in other faculties (Black, Jeffreys, & Hartley, 1993). While further study may be needed to assess the correlation between difficult early life experiences and the choice of social work as a career, it cannot be ignored as an important factor in the selection and preparation of candidates for professional training (Lafrance et al, 2004). When a professionally questionable behaviour emerges it is often first experienced in the small group tutorial. The tutor uses the opportunities to explore the professional practice implications of the behaviour. In the skills lab in particular, students also have an opportunity to view themselves on film and are facilitated to make the connections to good practice. If this fails the tutor will meet the student individually. This conversation often begins the process of self realisation leading to a decision to take time out or to transfer to the BASS. When rigorous attendance and behavioural requirements have been made explicit and contextualised to professional behaviours, there has been a marked improvement in attendance, assignment submissions and codes of behaviour.

Legal issues

Legal issues are the most commonly cited institutional obstacle to effective gatekeeping (Gibbs & Macy, 2000). Today's litigious society couples a conservative political climate with endangerment of resource allocation to dramatically compromise the commitment to gatekeeping. Foremost is the fear of legal action. Pressures from institutional administrators and their legal advisors were barriers identified to the development of sound policies and practices that support programmes to 'screen out' students who are not suitable for a career in social work. Institutions of higher education must accept that the implications of offering access to non-traditional students begin rather than end at the point of entry.

Providing an exit route

For the mature student the stakes for failing to complete the course successfully are very high. Prior to 2008, it was possible for a BSW student to reach year three or even the final year when a failed fieldwork placement resulted in no degree being awarded. This position appeared iniquitous in the extreme and suggested a degree of institutional oppression that rested uneasily with mission statements on access and social inclusion. There was a need to provide, as a matter of urgency, an alternative academic route for those deemed unsuitable for professional progression. The discourse of social inclusion seems relevant for addressing the contested issues of rights and responsibilities that arise. An inclusive response to the gatekeeping issues that arose on the BSW was to provide an exit route for those deemed unsuitable for professional training or who failed fieldwork practice placements. Consequently the Bachelor of Applied Social Studies (BASS) was inaugurated in 2008. This is purely an academic qualification and has no professional implications or obligations. The BASS route acknowledges students strengths and offers an alternative path to university qualification. The duty of care to all stakeholders is addressed by this initiative, which acknowledges issues of access and inclusion while protecting vulnerable service users. The issues that laid the foundation for the BASS exit route are among those commonly encountered when a tension exists in balancing professional standards with open access. These issues can militate against the development of clear procedures and actions to support the 'duty of care' aspect of professional formation. As a social work educator it is my responsibility to ensure that students whose impairments will interfere with their professional judgement and performance should be diverted towards the exit route. It is not enough to pass the buck in the hope that agency or professional licensing will stop those who are dangerous or harmful. In Ireland we know all too well, as recent enquiries and reports into clerical and institutional abuse attest, where that particular route has led. The current reality is that few social work programmes have well defined policies for non-admission or termination of students for reasons other than academic failure. A compelling argument can be made it seems that in professional programmes, appropriate professional behaviour should be viewed as an academic requirement rather than as a misconduct issue (Cobb & Jordan, 1989; Moore & Urwin, 1990). Research suggests that successful outcomes in this domain begin at the point of entry. Students are made aware that certain behaviours are expected and that others will not be tolerated. Additionally, the need for standardised assessment frameworks, that include professional behavioural requirements need to be included in Marks and Standards to support all colleagues, particularly those who are delivering courses from disciplines external to the professional context concerned. However, to sail safely between the Charybdis of professional formation and the Scylla of social inclusion, these Fitness to Practise Guidelines/Protocols need to be in place pre-course commencement in order to minimise the exclusionary effects of this provision.

Further reflections on using groupwork to gatekeep

At an institutional level there is a growing awareness that fitness to practise is an on-going issue for all professional and clinical programmes. The university has established a Fitness to Practise Group to develop guidelines and codes of conduct to ensure that professional standards are maintained though assessment and sanction in order to meet the challenges arising in professional and clinical education. This initiative is evidence of a shift in wider university policies recalibrating social inclusion and professional formation. The guidelines are likely to be protocol by late 2013.

The pathfinding role of groupwork in delivering multi-dimensional interventions that value other voices and alternative world views can be acknowledged from the UCC experience. It is the central element holding diverse interventions coherently together. It is the means by which contested issues can be raised and resolved. By valuing the practice wisdom of colleagues, practitioners, service users and students knowledge for best practice is built. This is an outcome that is not only desirable but possible for constructing humanistic responses to the issues that arise in the professional formation of the non-traditional student cohort. Gatekeeping is an on-going process of evolving ideas about what constitutes the common good. Groupwork for gatekeeping enables the collective exercise and exploration of the professional challenges that arise in delivering to that ideal.

Conclusion

The possibilities, challenges and outcomes that arise in maintaining professional standards in the delivery of professional social work education and training to non-traditional students have been explored in this paper. Thoughts evidencing the use of groupwork in gatekeeping, and in building collaborative relationships and inclusive structures that foster corporate responsibility with users, professionals and institutions, were reviewed as central to programme integrity. Future issues concerning access are likely to be contested as competing needs and rights are debated. The continued relevance and use of groupwork for this collective exploration must encourage us to be hopeful about the creative synergies that can be fostered by walking the talk!

References

Bamber, Anthony L. 1995. *Supporting adult learners,* London: Library Association.

Black, P.N., Jeffreys, D., & Hartley, E.K. (1993). Personal History of Psychosocial trauma in the early life of social work and business students in *Journal of Social Work Education 29:* 171-180.

Cobb,N., & Jordan,C. (1989). Students with questionable values or threatening behaviour: precedent and policy from discipline to dismissal, in *Journal of Social Work Education, 25 (2):87-97.*

Cowburn, M., Nelson, P., & Williams, J. (2000). Assessment of Social Work Students: standpoint and strong objectivity. In *Social Work Education,* 19 (6):627-637.

Elliott, T., Frazer, T., Garrard, D., Hickinbotham, J., Horton, V.,Mann, J.,Soper, S., Turner, J., Turner, M., & Whiteford, A. (2005). Practice learning and assessment on Social Work Service User Conversations. In *Social Work Education,* Vol 24, *No 4,* June 2005, 451-466.

Foley,G (2004). *Dimensions of Adult Learning,* UK: Open University Press.

Friere, P. (1973). *The Pedagogy of the Oppressed.* New York: Herder and Herder.

Gibbs, P., & Macy, H., (2000). The arena of gatekeeping. In *Gatekeeping in BSW Programs.* Patty Gibbs & Eleanor H. Blakely (eds) 2000. New York: Columbia University Press, 3-21.

Kolb, D. (1984). *Experiential Learning.* USA Englewood Cliffs: Prentice Hall.

Lafrance, J., Gray , E.,& Herbert, M. (2004) Gate-keeping for Professional Social Work Practice. *Social Work Education, 23(3): 325-340.*

Lee, J.A.B. (1994). *The Empowerment Approach to Social Work Practice.* New York: Columbia University Press.

Lordan, N., Wilson, M., and Quirke, D. (2009). Mask Making and Social Groupwork. In: *Strength and Diversity in Social Work with Groups.* Carol S. Cohen, Michael H Phillips and Meredith Hanson (eds). New York: Routledge.

Lordan, N., Wilson, M., & Quirke, D. (2007). Masks in Social Work. In: *Visual*

Practices across the University, Jim Elkins, (ed). Munchen: Wilhelm Fink Verlag.

Lordan, N. & Wilson, M. (2002). Groupwork in Europe: Tools to Combat Social Exclusion in a Multicultural Environmet. In: *Social Work with Groups: Mining the Gold.* Sue Henry, Jean East and Catheryne Schmitz (eds). New York: The Haworth Press.

Moore, L. & Urwin, C. (1990). Quality control in social work: the gatekeeping role in social work education. In: *Journal of Teaching in Social Work, 4 (1):113-128.*

National Social Work Qualifications Board (NSWQB) Handbook 2003. Dublin: NSWQB.

Parker, J. (2007). Disadvantage, stigma and anti-oppressive practice. In: *Social Work and Disadvantage* Burke, P. and Parker, J. (eds). London: Jessica Kingsley.

Preston-Shoot, M. (2007). *Effective Groupwork.* Basingstoke: Palgrave.

Saleeby, D. (2002). *The Strengths Perspective in Social Work Practice.* New York: Longman.

Sankaran, S. (2001). *Effective Change Management: Using Action Learning and Action Research,* Lismore NSW: Southern Cross University Press.

Smith, Mark. (2009). Developing critical conversations about practice. In: *Groupwork Research.* Oded Manor (ed). London: Whiting and Birch.

Wilson, M. & Quirke, D. (2009). Promoting Partnership and Empowerment through Groupwork: The way forward for social work education. In: *Social Professional Activity: The search for a minimum common denominator in difference.* Claire Dorrity and Peter Herrmann (eds). New York: Nova Science Publishers, Inc.

7
Developing a white anti-racism identity: A psycho-educational group model

Kathryn K. Berg & Shirley R. Simon

Introduction

This chapter describes and assesses a seven session psycho-educational group on anti-racism identity development for White European-American undergraduate students at a midwestern U.S. University. It is predicated on the premise that Whiteness can simultaneously privilege and harm White people, and that White students have the potential to become personally invested in challenging systematic racism. It is also based on the idea that a group structure presents an ideal format for addressing this topic. Peer support, a safe environment, and information are requisites for facilitating personal exploration of this sensitive subject. A group model for addressing this topic is presented and assessed. Key considerations, essential elements, strengths and weaknesses, suggestions for replication and further research are discussed.

Background

Racism can harm White European-Americans while it simultaneously privileges this same population. This is a challenging concept for many to grasp, including the typical White person in the United States who likely considers racism deplorable. While the consequences for White

European-Americans who challenge racism pale in comparison to the impact of systemic racism on people-of-color, Whites often have less incentive and less support systems readily available to motivate long-term racial justice advocacy. In order to empower Whites to develop their anti-racism capabilities, informational resources, emotional resilience, and support systems are needed to withstand any resulting social repercussions.

Whites are socialized to see racism not as a system, but as isolated behaviors enacted by highly unethical or uneducated people (Akintunde, 1999). In reality, racism is an everyday, commonplace occurrence. In order to effectively interrupt White supremacy, Whites require the willingness and emotional capacity to acknowledge and deal with the racist implications of their own thoughts and behaviors. When feelings of shame, anger, guilt, and denial are at the root of someone's racially problematic thought patterns, education and exposure alone are not sufficient interventions (Tochluk, 2008). Furthermore, to effect lasting change, White people must develop the capacity to effectively advocate for racial justice by challenging and supporting other Whites (Tatum, 1997). The interpersonal challenges that White European-Americans often face as they develop anti-racism identities, such as compromised support systems and immature defense mechanisms, also need to be addressed in order to eliminate racism.

Some anti-racism educators assert that the most prevalent and insidious form of racism in present day society is "color-blindness" (Wise, 2010). Often, White European-Americans are socialized to think that acknowledging someone's race is inherently racist. In fact, the opposite is true: to fail to see someone's race is to neglect to understand the role that systemic racism plays in that person's life (Kendall, 2006). For Whites, this largely stems from a lack of understanding of the impact that Whiteness has on their lives. Consequently, White European-Americans normalize and maintain Whiteness as the status quo. The antidote for this color-blindness is helping Whites develop a racial identity. When Whites can truly understand the role of race in their own lives and in society as a whole, they have a greater capacity to interrupt racism (Helms, 1992; Okun, n.d.).

A group format is an ideal model for fostering racial identity development for White European-Americans. By providing a safe, supportive environment for interactions with peers around this sensitive topic, a group can enable the honest exploration and reflection necessary for participants' growth and development. Sharing the often painful processes of self-assessment, acceptance of personal responsibility and commitment to change with those who are similar in race, age, and educational level provides the universality and hope that can facilitate change. As members learn about and explore racial justice with White European-American leaders and peers, they can come to appreciate that Whites need to assume responsibility for educating other Whites about racial injustice, and can, in fact, practice the interpersonal skills to do so. Moreover, providing this experience and training to college or university age students may capitalize on the opportunity to influence a population that is typically open to self-assessment and personal reflection.

A group model of support

A White identity development group was initiated at an urban, midwestern University. It aimed to provide White European-American undergraduate students with information, support, and encouragement to address racial injustice. Based upon a number of conceptual frameworks discussed later in this paper, as well as diversity materials already developed by the University's Center for Student Diversity, a curricular model on anti-racism training for White undergraduate students was created with the purpose of engaging these students in the Center's mission of multiculturalism. The Center for Student Diversity funded a pilot group based on this model. By offering training and support to White students with a strong interest in anti-racism, it was hoped that they, in turn, would educate peers within their racial group and hold them accountable for racial justice.

Goals of the group

This section discusses the curricular model and learning outcomes of the seven session psycho-educational group on White identity development. The model was grounded in the principles and practices of effective social group work, including universalization, mutual aid and peer support (Drumm, 2006). There were three key goals for the group. The first was to provide White European-American undergraduate students with additional skills, information, and supports so that they could act as more effective allies for people-of-color. The second was for the student-participants to explore the impact of Whiteness on themselves, their families, and their communities in the interest of understanding how racism both privileges and harms Whites. Third, the group aimed to help student-participants learn that they, as White European-Americans, are responsible for holding other Whites accountable for racial justice, without being experts on the lived experience of racial oppression.

Overall, the major learning outcomes for the training were divided into three categories: knowledge, values, and skills. With regard to knowledge, it was anticipated that student-participants would be able to define systematic racism, describe the history of Whiteness, situate their families within that history, and describe their personal experiences of White privilege. Furthermore, participants would be able to identify examples of exemplary past and present White racial justice allies, individuals who have demonstrated an outstanding commitment to anti-racism work, often at great risk, throughout their career. In the area of values, it was hoped that participants would appreciate the concept of a healthy White anti-racism identity, understand their own experiences as members of a White racial group, and actively promote racial justice by engaging in respectful, constructive discussion of racial micro-aggressions, or individual instances in which people-of-color experience the discriminatory effects of racism. With regard to skills, the group aimed to help participants utilize new strategies to identify and interrupt racial micro-aggressions in their daily lives, demonstrate interpersonal skills for building relationships with White racial justice advocates, and utilize techniques for enhancing self-awareness regarding White identity development. Please see Table 1 for a summary of these objectives.

Recruitment

The primary recruitment method was class visitations with professors whose coursework incorporated issues of social justice. Most participants were recruited through brief, five to ten minute class presentations about the group. This strategy was based upon the premise that direct contact with prospective group members is an effective way of recruiting participants (Toseland & Rivas, 2012). The leader was introduced as a representative of the Center for Student Diversity,

Table 1. Summary of knowledge, values, and skills objectives

Knowledge
Provide examples of exemplary White racial justice allies in history and the present
Define systematic racism and situate one's personal experience of White privilege
Describe the history of Whiteness and situate one's family within that history

Values
Appreciate the importance of a healthy White anti-racism identity
Be able to reframe one's experiences within the context of membership in a White racial group
Appreciate the need for respectful, constructive discussion of racial micro-aggressions

Skills
Use new tools to identify and interrupt racial micro-aggressions in one's daily life
Use new tools for self-awareness to progress in one's White identity development
Demonstrate interpersonal skills for building relationships with White racial justice allies

promoting a new program entitled, *What's it like to be White? White identity development and anti-racism training.* The training group was described as an opportunity for White European-American students to learn about "Whiteness" and to have conversations about racial justice. The facilitator explained that challenging racism can be a difficult and emotionally trying experience, and this group would provide a supportive environment for gaining information, self-awareness, and practical skills for interrupting racism. The facilitator provided information about the curriculum and application procedures, and answered students' questions. Copies of the flier and application form were distributed. Additional recruitment tools included the distribution of fliers and presentations to student organizations.

Conceptual frameworks

A number of conceptual frameworks provided the foundation for this pilot project: social group work principles; person-in-environment perspective; cognitive-behavioral theory; and two White identify development models.

The principles of effective group work provided an overarching framework for the training. Yalom's (2005) therapeutic factors served as an ongoing foundation for group intervention. Cohesion, a critical component of effective groups, was consciously encouraged throughout the seven sessions. Fostering universality was also critical to facilitate a safe, open environment as participants developed a growing sense of themselves as members of the same racial group and explored the sensitive issues evoked by this training. Being amongst racial peers gave the members permission to share honestly and to view themselves non-defensively. Interpersonal learning was observed as members gained insight and self-awareness during the here-and-now moments of the group discussion. Imparting information, in both the more formal didactic form and direct advice from members, was, of course, a critical component of the group process. The presentations by guest experts as well as the sharing of ideas among the members provided essential information and perspectives.

Issues of group development were also a concern. Beginning considerations of safety, trust, contracting and participation were particularly essential given the sensitive nature of the subject. Middle stage issues included facilitation and clarification of process and incorporation of appropriate programmatic activities. Effective closure strategies to maintain and implement the goals of the group were also important. As in most groups, the role of the leader was critical to its success. For this group, the role of the leader as facilitator, role model, and "non-hierarchical expert" was also crucial (Yalom, 2005; Bernstein, 1973; Berman-Rossi, 1993).

In addition, the model incorporated the person-in-environment framework and cognitive-behavioral theory. The person-in-environment perspective allowed student-participants to situate their personal experiences within a broader perspective of systematic racism. While the group members gained an understanding of the various forms of racism and the different ways that it is maintained, it was also recognized that the members had been socialized to uphold systems of White supremacy (Monkman, 1991). The group incorporated cognitive-behavioral theory to support students in altering thought patterns and defenses that perpetuate racism (Magen, 2009). In order for student-participants to view racial tensions through an anti-racism lens, members explored how thought patterns influence emotional reactions to racially charged topics and events. Cognitive-behavioral techniques, such as reframing, were incorporated. Support for changes in identity development was provided throughout the training.

Finally, two White identity development models by Janet Helms and Tema Okun served as foundations for understanding the stages of growth leading to a healthy White anti-racism identity. Janet Helm's (1992) six stage model is frequently referenced in the literature, and is useful in understanding White identity development and the transitional stages between a state of "color-blindness" and White anti-racism identity. Tema Okun (n.d.) identifies nine stages that lead to actively becoming anti-racist and subsequently maintaining that identity as part of a life-long effort. Material from both of these authors was shared with the group.

Structure of the group

The group required a minimum of six students and was capped at a maximum of twelve. This size was thought to be small enough to allow time for everyone to contribute to each discussion, but large enough to include diversity in strengths, perspective, and experience (Toseland & Rivas, 2012). There were seven group sessions, each two hours long. It was believed that this length of time would be sufficient to achieve learning outcomes while accommodating the competing scheduling demands of the student-participants. Dinner was provided fifteen minutes before the sessions began with members allowed to continue eating during the first half of the session. By providing dinner, the facilitator addressed one of the practical considerations of the time slot while simultaneously creating a nurturing environment. Meetings were held in a small, private room in the campus union thereby maximizing confidentiality.

In order to identify changes in comprehension of key concepts as well as participants' self-assessments of their achievement of the learning objectives, pre- and post-test surveys were administered to all participants. The surveys consisted of a series of 14 questions using a five-point Likert scale, plus one open-ended question on the post-test requesting respondents to identify their most important learning. These surveys received approval from the Institutional Review Board of the sponsoring university.

Participants were provided with a booklet of readings, homework exercises, and a journal to foster ongoing growth outside of the actual meetings. All sessions opened with a brief presentation and discussion of an exemplary White ally from the past or present. These allies served as models that group members could look to for inspiration. The sessions typically closed with a relaxation exercise as a vehicle for transitioning from the group to their everyday activities. Group sessions were loosely divided between presentation of content and processing of material. Participants were asked to read assigned articles and respond to reflection questions in a journal between sessions. Most sessions included discussion of these journal entries.

The topics for each meeting were ordered in a sequence intended to foster the development of the group as-a-whole as well as the White anti-racism identity of each participant. The purpose of session one was to begin to develop group cohesion and trust, and to establish a contract with ground rules for creating an anti-oppression atmosphere. Session two introduced participants to the process of White identity development. Sessions three and four examined systematic racism, providing opportunities to begin or continue linking "the personal to the political." Session five encouraged participants to support one another in working through feelings of guilt, anger, and shame. Sessions six and seven focused on strategies for interrupting racism in the larger society. Please see Table 2 for specific topics, readings, and reflection questions for each session.

The groupworker who facilitated the pilot study did not hold any additional academic or extra-curricular authority over group participants. The group leader had a background in feminist theory and societal power structures. She worked as a program coordinator at the Center for Student Diversity for one semester prior to conducting the pilot group. The curricular model was developed by the groupworker at the request of and with consultation from Center staff.

Table 2
Weekly topic, readings, and reflection questions

Session One: Foundations for Anti-Racism Community
"Embracing a Cross-Racial Dialogue" by Beverly Daniel Tatum
(Chapter ten from *Why Are All the Black Kids Sitting Together in the Cafeteria*)
What motivates you to learn about issues of racial injustice?

Session Two: White Identity Development
"From White Racist to White Anti-Racist" by Tema Okun
When did you realize you were White? Where are you in your own process of
White identity development?

Session Three: The History of Whiteness
"Uncovering a Hidden History" by Shelly Tochluk (Chapter three from
Witnessing Whiteness: First steps toward an antiracist practice and culture)
Reflect on your family history as it relates to your family's experience of
Whiteness. When did your family become White? What ways did they, or have
they, experienced their race and ethnicity? In what ways is their experience
different from and/or similar to your individual experience of race and ethnicity?

Session Four: Racism as Systematic
"White Privilege: Unpacking the Invisible Knapsack" by Peggy McIntosh
Journal about how you react to your Whiteness on a daily basis. Describe your
experiences of being consciously White. Come up with at least ten examples
of how being White is part of your lived experience.

Session Five: Self-Reflection and Working through Guilt
"The Egalitarian Brain" by David Amodio
Has your experience of White privilege ever had a detrimental impact on
relationships with people that you value? Has your experience of White privilege
ever limited your self-awareness? Reflect on one or more times when this was
the case. What have you learned since then?

Session Six: Identifying Racial Micro-aggression
"How White People Can Serve as Allies to People of Color in the Struggle to
End Racism" by Paul Kivel
What have your experiences with racial micro-aggression, from a position of
White privilege, made you feel like? When you have witnessed racism, what
was that experience like? If you have attempted to interrupt or "call out" racism,
what was that like for you? What have you learned since then?

Session Seven: Turning Knowledge into Action
"Resistance" by Tim Wise (Chapter four from *White Like Me*)
What is the most important thing you have learning from participating in the
White Identity Development and Anti-Racism Training?

The pilot program

Once the initial plans had been developed, the pilot program was implemented during the ensuing spring semester under the auspices of the University's Center for Student Diversity. Each session had specific learning objectives which are summarized in Table 3.

Table 3
Weekly learning objectives

Session One: Foundations for Anti-Racism Community
Develop the skills needed for creating a safe space
Recognize oneself as a White person within a White context
Be able to use empathy and reframing as tools for self-awareness in increasing one's capacities as a White ally

Session Two: White Identity Development
Understand the stages of White identity development
Recognize emotions that influence stages of White identity development
Recognize oneself within the stages of White identity development

Session Three: The History of Whiteness
Recognize that Whiteness is a social construct invented with a political agenda
Gain basic knowledge about the history behind the concept of Whiteness
Situate one's family history within a history of Whiteness

Session Four: Racism as Systematic
Understand the concept of racism as systemic
Identify daily experiences of White privilege
Understand how one's daily experiences fit into larger systems

Session Five: Self-Reflection and Working through Guilt
Learn how to support fellow White allies in working through their own guilt
Gain greater understanding as to how one's experience is shared by others
Learn how to turn "guilt into gratitude" and use the perspective of "situated action" as tools for increasing self-awareness

Session Six: Identifying Racial Micro-aggression
Learn how to recognize a racial micro-aggression
Learn methods of interrupting systematic racism
Learn techniques for recognizing and interrupting racial micro-aggressions

Session Seven: Turning Knowledge into Action
Learn how to use knowledge from the training to further racial justice as part of a racially diverse community
Identify expectations for continued effort as a White racial justice ally
Identify additional resources and supports for continued work as a White racial justice ally

Session One

Session one was entitled "Foundation for Anti-Racism Community." The purposes of this session were to begin fostering group cohesion, create a contractual agreement for group interactions, and establish a safe environment for future interactions. The group created and agreed upon a list of ground rules during the first session which included being an active listener, asking questions rather than confronting, speaking up if a comment made one uncomfortable, and arriving on time, prepared to participate in the group.

The leader recognized that while participants expected to find the group challenging, they needed to be assured of a supportive environment in which one need not feel ashamed or embarrassed. The sessions, therefore, took place in a comfortable, private, conveniently-located room and fostered what Dessel, Rogge, and Garlington (2006) define as intergroup dialogue work, where, "[Participants] are encouraged to collaborate willingly, be vulnerable, and believe in the authenticity of all participants." Group members seemed to approach the training with this mindset.

During week one, group members participated in introductions and several icebreakers. These included a "name chant," in which group members quickly passed a ball around the circle while saying their own name. It was followed by a ball toss game, in which participants called out the name of the person to whom they were about to toss the ball. Next, they participated in an exercise called "common ground." The participants split into two groups, where members were asked to identify traits that they shared in common and report this to the larger group. Finally, members were asked to write their personal goals for the training on a piece of paper. They inserted these papers into envelopes and were asked to seal the envelopes and write their names on them, so that the goals could be returned to the respective members at the end of the training.

After a brief break, there was an explanation of binary systems of oppression, hierarchies in which a dichotomy is socially constructed with the effect of privileging one group at the expense of another. Next, there was a group activity in which members were asked to list different binary systems of oppression, such as gender, religion, age, and sexual orientation. The leader discussed how each system of oppression was equally worthy of attention; however this training would focus on the topic of race. The leader introduced two cognitive tools aimed at supporting the group throughout the training: empathy and reframing. Using empathy, a White person can tap into her/his experiences of oppression, or lack of privilege, in other areas of identity, as a means of relating to people-of-color. The second skill, "reframing," is a method of altering the way we view an experience. For example, "Affirmative action prevents Whites from receiving equal opportunities," could be reframed as, "Affirmative action is an effort to address the fact that Whites have unearned advantages due to racism."

Session Two

Session two focused on the subject of White identity development. To begin this session, participants re-entered the group environment by repeating the ball toss game. Next, they played an interactive, cohesion-building game of "interpersonal bingo" in which participants received a bingo card listing characteristics of participants and tried to place the names of the participants in the corresponding boxes. (The leader had designed these cards prior to the session.) Following these two experiential activities, the facilitator discussed how this type of training might raise issues of personal growth and/or stress for the participants, and explained that additional support was available through the University's Wellness Center. A guest counselor from the Wellness Center then described the Center and its services. Next, the group viewed a film entitled *The Color of Fear*, and participants shared a "snap-shot reaction" or one-sentence response to the film. To close the session, the guest counselor led the students in a loving-kindness meditation, which allowed them to practice self-soothing through visualization and the cultivation of forgiveness towards self and others.

During sessions one and two, students were very receptive and engaged. Many students shared important and potentially vulnerable aspects of their identities as early as the first hour of the training. This allowed the group to progress through the pre-affiliation stage quickly and easily (Garland, Jones & Kolodny, 1973), which could be attributed to the voluntary, self-selected membership of the group.

Session Three

Session three, entitled, "The history of Whiteness" featured a presentation by a guest speaker on systematic racism. The presentation explained how the social construct or perception of Whiteness, as Americans know it today, was historically invented with a political agenda. Participants were very engaged by the interactive presentation, with some shedding tears upon seeing the cover of a 1939 issue of Time Magazine proclaiming Hitler

"Man of the Year." The presentation concluded with a more contemporary discussion about the race of an actor from the television show "Glee," a woman born in South Korea and adopted into a White-European American family at three months old.

This presentation was followed by an activity in which participants used an adapted sociogram exercise, a graphic drawing of the generational lineage of their families, to share when their families first became White European-Americans. This activity aimed to personalize the concept of a "family history of Whiteness." Group members individually created family trees which incorporated a "family myth," or one unspoken family rule, as well as one word descriptors for various individuals, or branches of the family. The group members drew extensive charts. One participant was a refugee from Eastern Europe whose recent family was a victim of genocide; another had family members in the South whose ancestors were slave owners; and another participant's ancestry was literally traced back to the landing of the Mayflower in 1620. One group member, a first generation immigrant whose family came from Greece, found the exercise particularly challenging. The student had not yet discerned how her strong ethnic identity was connected to her experience of race. It was hoped that by creating and presenting sociograms, group members could begin to see the broader connections and to view themselves as members of a White racial group with diverse cultural influences.

Session Four

Session four, entitled "Racism as Systemic" featured a presentation by a guest speaker discussing the history of our criminal justice system. By examining the criminal justice system, the speaker was able to convey the different levels on which racism has operated in the history of United States law enforcement and continues to do so. Participants were given pieces of paper describing specific historical moments of racial injustice, and were asked as a group to place them in chronological sequence. Group members had the chance to respond to the presentation, with one participant noting the racism that underlies the difference in penalties for possessing crack versus powder cocaine. By the end of this presentation, it was hoped that group members could better understand and appreciate that racism operates on a systemic level beyond the mere interactions of individuals.

Following the presentation, the leader asked group members to share examples of how they experienced Whiteness in their daily lives. The topic had been assigned as a journal question, and group members did an excellent job of identifying experiences of White privilege in their daily lives. One recognized that ease in obtaining employment was in part due to racial privilege. Another shared that her behaviors might easily have led to jail as a high school student if she had been a person-of-color. One group member noted that strangers on the bus would more often choose the neighboring empty space, as opposed to the one next to people-of-color. Group members were then asked to name possible examples of how racism was harmful to White people. This question was more challenging for the group. While some participants appeared to grasp the concept easily, others struggled to understand how this was possible. One student thought it overly indulgent to examine the effects of racism on White people. Yet, as a group, members were able to share pertinent examples. These included a general lack of cultural competency, feelings of being socially awkward in racially diverse settings, an incident of presumed class privilege due to racial privilege, and the premise that White women are arguably under-tested for some STDs by health providers. The supportive, trusting group atmosphere facilitated the development of intimacy, interpersonal learning, enhanced personal reflection, and permission to explore this challenging topic. There was no overt interpersonal conflict evidenced throughout the training.

Session Five

Session five, entitled "Self-reflection and working through guilt," was devoted to discussing personal experiences with racial micro-aggressions, or those daily experiences of racism that collectively contribute to White privilege. This session opened with students reading quotes distributed by the leader addressing the subject of guilt in regard to racism. For example, a quotation by Tochluck (2008) read, "To begin honestly, we must discuss what may be, for White people, the most challenging aspect of any discussion of race. We must deal with the terms *racist, racism,* and *systemic White supremacy.* We must also confront the fact that some people might ask us to associate those words with ourselves and our actions" (Tochluk, 2008). It was hoped that this quote in particular would validate and normalize any anxieties that student-participants felt about exploring personal experiences of perpetuating racism. Members responded by sharing personal examples of the relevance that the quotation held for them.

Group members were then asked to share examples of when systematic racism had limited their self-awareness or been detrimental to their relationships. One group member questioned the value of this discussion, distinguishing racism on the individual level from large-scale social change. The leader then challenged the group members to consider the relationships between individuals and institutions. She asked them to think about their career aspirations and to consider the connection between their roles in institutions and their ability to impact social systems.

The increased comfort and trust that had been developed by week five allowed for deeper and the more challenging exploration of racially problematic thought patterns in the here-and-now. The leader began by sharing a recent micro-aggression she had committed. To some of the members, this incident sounded relatively minor and did not appear to have a strong negative impact. Two members responded by insisting that the act had not been racist. The leader explained that although the action was well-intended and did not appear to cause offense, it could still be considered racist. This exchange highlighted the value of having a White European-American person lead the group in order to demonstrate how racism could be fostered by relatively benign actions and how Whites have a responsibility to acknowledge and learn from these actions. It also set the stage for another group member to share a personal experience that evoked feelings of vulnerability.

Next, one student shared the use of "reframing" to understand affirmative action. Initially, the student was bitter about not being accepted into Ivy League colleges, especially when compared to a Black woman, featured in the local newspaper, who had similar accomplishments but was admitted to these schools. The student explained that looking back, it was now easier to appreciate the role of affirmative action in balancing an unlevel playing field, and yet, on a personal level, she still struggled with this concept. The other students proceeded to share their own frustrations with affirmative action, especially as it applies to the college application process. One student asserted that it was the one situation in which race should not be taken into account. The leader posed some questions that challenged these assertions and, as a result, members shared their willingness to re-examine these views. The participants appeared to experience some sort of connection and solace around this shared experience. The leader followed up on this discussion by e-mailing articles regarding the role of affirmative action.

The leader provided the group with a few strategies to help work through 'White guilt' in order to promote personal growth and social change. For instance, they were told how "turning guilt into gratitude" is a way of valuing the things that we have in our lives to be thankful for and that can help us to maintain our anti-racism efforts, rather than simply experiencing guilt (Van Dernoot Lipsky, 2009). Members were also invited to think about "situated action," or the ability to reach White people who would be more receptive to other Whites than to people-of-color. At the end of the session, participants received "racial justice Tic-tacs," Tic-tacs with the original label removed and replaced with one that read, "Take one to move through guilt towards action." These served as a humorous reminder for the need to transform guilt into positive social action.

Between Sessions Five and Six

Between sessions five and six, group members were asked to respond to a series of three questions as part of an asynchronous online discussion in which everyone sent an e-mail to the group at their own convenience during the week. This ensured that all group members obtained similar information regardless of attendance, which was anticipated to be lower during weeks five and six (due to pre-scheduled commitments). It also allowed participants who more comfortably expressed themselves in writing to share their perspectives with the group. Members responded to the following questions: 1) For what reasons is it generally taboo for the average White person to 'call out' behaviors that we perceive as racist (especially with Whites that we respect or even love)? 2) What feelings would such behaviors provoke for you and/or other White people you know? 3) How does this White American cultural norm, of not addressing racism when it is occurring, prevent Whites from doing racial justice ally work? The three questions were an opportunity for participants to begin to understand the primary role of the White ally, which "is not to help victims of racism, but to speak up against systems of oppression and challenge other Whites [sic.] to do the same" (Tatum, 1997).

This asynchronous online exercise gave students the opportunity to learn from one another and to share their ideas without feeling put on the spot. It was a space in which group members explored the link between their emotions around racism and their ability to interrupt racial micro-aggressions. This interactive online component seemed well-received and was a valuable aspect of the training model, providing an opportunity to explore the link between one's emotions regarding racism and one's ability to interrupt racial micro-aggression.

Session Six

Session six, entitled "Identifying racial micro-aggression," featured a guest presentation on the emotional impact of racial micro-aggressions regularly experienced by people-of-color. Following this presentation, the group engaged in a discussion about racial micro-aggressions. Group members were asked to share either an experience in which they interrupted a racial micro-aggression, or an awareness of someone else effectively interrupting a racial micro-aggression. By now, the group's trust and comfort had developed sufficiently to allow members to safely open up and share honestly about these risky actions. One group member shared an example of how she became aware of her own unconscious racial micro-aggressions. Two other participants shared personal experiences of calling out racism, both describing their actions as courageous. This open sharing led to a group discussion about strategies for effectively responding to racism in the future.

Session Seven

"Turning knowledge into action," the topic for session seven, picked up on the discussion of session six, addressing the limitations of personal change without a long-term effort to effect social change. Staff who had a role in supporting the training and students who had recently attended a White privilege conference were invited to join the group as guests for part of this final meeting. It was hoped that this presence would create a link to future resources by introducing the group to a larger, racially diverse community working on issues of anti-racism. This session included a "White ethnic food potluck." Group members were asked to bring a dish reflecting one of their ethnic heritages with additional White ethnic food ordered for the event. The guest speaker addressed the importance of having communities supportive of anti-racism while attempting to educate and impact our spheres of influence. Group members were encouraged to practice "calling out" racism with trusted friends and family. At the end of the session, participants shared one or two personal commitments to furthering racial justice in their own lives while guests shared hopes and expectations for those completing the training.

The leader helped to conclude the group by providing a summary and review of the accomplishments of the group over the past seven weeks. She affirmed that leaving the group with unanswered questions was a testament to the growth of the members. The leader distributed gift bags that included a hand-written card acknowledging an individual member's strength and a quote by a Maori woman: "If you have come here to help me, you are wasting your time. But if you have come because your liberation is bound up with mine, then we can work together." In order to facilitate future growth, the gift bags also included a checklist detailing the qualities of effective White racial justice advocates. Lastly, the gift bags contained an anti-racism travel mug which featured a humorous, neon-colored cartoon image that read "Anti-Racism: A White on White Responsibility." Activities of the final session were aimed at facilitating separation and helping individual members transition to continued action without the group's support.

Initial assessment

The pilot group consisted of seven female university participants. All were traditional-age students (eighteen to twenty-two) with the exception of one graduate student member in her mid-twenties. The group was heterogeneous in many areas including year in school, academic area of study, home city/location, sexual orientation, religious affiliation, geographic home, and ethnic background. Three of the participants were psychology majors with the remaining four representing music, biology, political science and women's and gender studies. All participants began the training with at least a basic level of awareness about their own racial privilege. Many identified the goal of gaining increased skills to advocate for racial justice as a desired outcome of the group experience.

Data gathered through assessments on the pre- and post-test instruments as well as through process observations provided the basis for an initial assessment of the pilot group experience. Each of the instruments included two identical sections with the post-test containing one additional open-ended question: What is the most important thing you have learned from participating in the White Identity Development and Anti-Racism Training? The first section asked each participant to rate their degree of understanding of seven different concepts. The seven concepts were: 1) white identity development, 2) whiteness as a political construct, 3) systematic racism, 4) racial micro-aggressions, 5) white privilege, 6) being a member of a white racial group and 7) being a white racial justice ally. For each statement, students selected one of the following four responses: 1 - completely understand, 2 - moderately understand, 3 - do not understand very well and 4 - do not understand at all. In the second section the students were asked to indicate their level of agreement with the following 7 statements: 1) I understand my identity and culture and the impact it has on my relationships with others, 2) I appreciate new ideas and cultures, 3) I do not suppress racist thoughts and instead find healthy ways of addressing them and unlearning racism, 4) I am confident in my ability to identify and interrupt racial micro-aggressions, 5) I am able to comfortably engage in respectful, constructive discussion of racial micro-aggressions with other white people, 6) I am able to identify exemplary white racial justice allied in history and in present times, and 7) I have the skills to work through feelings of guilt and confusion in order to act in the interest of racial justice. They were asked to rate each statement from 1-5, where one meant strongly agree and 5 indicated strongly disagree. The individual scores for each question are presented in Tables 4 and 5.

The responses to the items on the first section of the post-test indicated that on average students demonstrated increased understanding for each of the seven statements. The average response to all statements was a three on the pre-test and a one on the post-test. The item that demonstrated the

Table 4

Pre- and post-test results: Understanding concepts

To what degree do you understand the following concepts? (1= high/4 = low)								
Concepts	Student Responses							Mean
White identity development	Pre	3	2	1	3	2	2	3	2.29
	Post	2	1	1	1	1	2	1	1.29
Whiteness as a political construct	Pre	2	4	4	4	2	2	3	3.00
	Post	1	2	1	1	1	1	1	1.14
Systematic racism	Pre	2	2	1	2	2	3	3	2.14
	Post	2	1	1	1	1	2	1	1.29
Racial micro-aggressions	Pre	3	3	4	4	2	2	2	2.86
	Post	1	1	1	1	1	1	2	1.14
White privilege	Pre	2	3	3	3	3	2	2	2.57
	Post	2	1	1	2	2	1	1	1.43
Being a member of a white racial group	Pre	2	3	2	4	2	2	2	2.43
	Post	1	2	1	2	1	1	1	1.29
Being a white racial justice ally	Pre	3	3	2	4	2	2	3	2.71
	Post	2	2	1	2	1	2	2	1.71

largest increase was the concept "Whiteness as a Political Construct." Every student indicated a higher level of agreement with all seven statements in the post-test when compared to the pre-test responses. The overall average of the differences in the second part of the surveys was one point. For the pre-test the average response was two while in the post-test the overall average was one. The largest growth was in response to the statement "I appreciate new ideas and cultures." Please see Table 4 and 5 for responses to specific items.

It was anticipated that students would gain valuable knowledge to support their individual processes of white identity development and social activism. The pre and post surveys did indicate an increase in students'

Table 4
Pre- and post-test results: Personal agreement with statements

Number that best indicates your level of agreement with the following statements (1 = agree/ 5 = disagree)								
Statements	Student responses							Mean
I understand my identity and culture and the impact it has on my relationships with others.	Pre	1	1	1	1	2	5	3	2.00
	Post	1	1	1	2	1	2	1	1.29
I appreciate new ideas and cultures.	Pre	4	1	3	4	4	4	3	3.29
	Post	1	1	2	1	1	2	1	1.29
I do not suppress racist thoughts and instead find healthy ways of addressing them and un-learning racism.	Pre	1	1	2	4	1	4	1	2.00
	Post	1	1	2	1	1	2	1	1.29
I am confident in my ability to identify and interrupt racial micro-aggressions.	Pre	3	1	2	2	1	5	1	2.14
	Post	2	1	1	2	2	2	1	1.57
I am able to comfortably engage in respectful, constructive discussion of racial micro-aggressions with other White people.	Pre	2	1	2	2	2	4	3	2.29
	Post	2	1	2	2	2	2	1	1.71
I am able to identify exemplary White racial justice allies in history and present times.	Pre	2	1	2	4	3	2	2	2.29
	Post	2	1	2	2	2	2	2	1.86
I have the skills to work through feelings of guilt and confusion in order to act in the interest of racial justice.	Pre	2	1	3	2	2	2	2	2.00
	Post	2	1	2	1	1	1	2	1.43

knowledge and awareness of opportunities for interrupting systematic racism. Within the pilot group session, participants demonstrated increased understanding of White privilege by effectively identifying instances of White privilege in their daily lives. They articulated connections between individual actions and larger social institutions, identifying opportunities to advocate for racial justice. One participant remarked,

Through this training I have learned about the effects of racism on an individual, group, and systematic level... Not only has this program helped me to work beyond guilt and towards action, but it has also given me the determination to start anti-racism initiatives within my [campus] and home communities.

Furthermore, students demonstrated increased knowledge about the history of Whiteness and were able to situate their families within that history. Participants demonstrated an increase in their understanding of Whiteness as a social construct. They recognized that the concept of Whiteness was created with a political agenda, and that their ancestors at some point became White European-Americans. One group member explained, "By further understanding my Whiteness and my White heritage, I feel that I can better communicate ideas of race and oppression to those that share my racial identity as well as express my commitment to anti-racism to those who are not my race." Such comments support the achievement of one of the primary objectives of the training – the development of the participants' White identities.

With regard to values, many group members indicated a greater commitment to anti-racism social change efforts. During the last session of the training, participants shared one or two goals for furthering racial justice in their lives. One group member, employed by the university as a Resident Advisor, planned to do additional outreach to residents-of-color during the upcoming school year. Another committed to discussing issues of racism with a parent. Students also demonstrated growth in the areas of personal awareness and self-acceptance. It is not uncommon for Whites who are opposed to racism to reject a racial identity altogether. However, as one participant stated, "I now know that it is very important for me to try to be myself and not to be ashamed of being White." Another group member gained greater comfort and ability to discuss racism, stating, "I have learned that it's okay to talk about racism in a way that benefits everyone, and that talking about it will improve knowledge and decrease White ignorance of the oppressions people-of-color face."

In the area of skills development, the group members acquired specific tools that allowed them to advocate for racial justice. Some of these skills were cognitive-behavioral techniques in which students learned how to reframe their own thought patterns. For example, during session five, two students, who initially expressed opposition to affirmative action, later spoke about their willingness to re-examine these views. Students also demonstrated new interpersonal capabilities. During session six, participants consulted with one another about strategies for interrupting racism in their daily lives. One self-identified introvert shared that, "It is very easy to keep my beliefs to myself, but in order to be a racial justice ally, I must speak up and take risks in order to help make a difference." Another group member, whose social networks almost exclusively represented people-of-color, learned the importance of engaging in conversation with other Whites: "I realized that I was unable to truly become a White ally until I engaged in conversation about race and ethnicity with White individuals [sic.]." Both students were able to identify new ways of promoting racial justice in their lives.

Discussion

This model, implemented as a pilot project, appears to have potential for facilitating anti-racism identity. It aimed to increase participants' knowledge, values, and skills with regard to racial justice advocacy. The training sought to empower students who were ready and willing to exert a greater anti-racism impact upon their campus community. Since this was a self-selected group, it seems logical that these students would be more open and knowledgeable than the typical undergraduate student. However, while they may have had greater intellectual knowledge about racism, they still lacked skills and resources to effect change among their peers and communities.

With regard to the objectives for the training, it appears that some success was achieved. At the outset of the group, participants were largely unaware of their own abilities to influence and promote racial justice advocacy. By the end of the training, all participants were exposed to new perspectives, strategies, and skills for interrupting racism and promoting racial justice within their lives. Students acquired new skills to explain systematic racism, situate their families within the historical construct of Whiteness, and relate personal experiences with White privilege. They were introduced to White racial justice allies with whom they were previously unfamiliar. By virtue of their ongoing participation in a formal White anti-racism group, participants became increasingly conscious of their membership in a White racial group and the opportunities to develop anti-racist identities. Group members achieved the goal of engaging in respectful, constructive discussions of racial micro-aggression during sessions five and six. While none of the group members were well-acquainted with one another prior to the training, they demonstrated interpersonal skills for building relationships with White racial justice allies by creating a supportive environment for one another. Finally, during session seven, when participants shared personal goals for continuing work in this area, participants identified and committed to ongoing, meaningful anti-racist activities.

Although the sample for this practice-evaluation is limited to a pilot group with seven participants, data suggest that the potential of the model warrants replication. The social work profession is committed to being at the forefront of social justice, and this model could contribute to its efforts to promote racial justice. The model goes beyond a basic education about the oppression of people-of-color and addresses issues of White guilt and the subtleties of racism in daily life; it challenges Whites to recognize, reflect upon, and educate others about the harm that racism inflicts upon White European-Americans like themselves.

Recommendations

Based upon this pilot group experience, recommendations for replication include:

- Expand the length of each session from two hours to two-and-a-half or three hours, and the number of sessions from seven to ten. This additional time would provide opportunities for developing long-term change and allow for critical topics and personal responses to be explored in greater depth.
- Add a session or module early in the training about how racism harms White people, distinguishing harm to Whites from systematic oppression of people-of-color. Within the pilot, there was inadequate time and attention given to this important premise.

- Include the topic of affirmative action as part of the curriculum of session five. When group members raised the subject during this session, it proved to be a very rich and meaningful topic for participants.
- Add a session or module on intersecting oppressed identities. It can be especially challenging for White students with additional oppressed identities, such as class, gender, sexual orientation, or religion, to separate and appreciate unique aspects of racism.
- Add a module or session devoted to the application of participants' new understandings of racism to their own campus environments. Provide statistics about racial-ethnic data on participants' home campuses.
- Be aware of the university calendar when scheduling the training sessions. For example, given the pressures of the final weeks of class, it could improve attendance to conclude the group several weeks before the end of the semester.
- Add video and audio materials to the curriculum as an alternative to guest speakers, if guest speakers are unavailable.

Conclusion

This group model appears to have the potential for impacting and encouraging growth and change. It harnesses the power of effective group work to facilitate the understanding that racism is unhealthy for all individuals, not just people-of-color. The group training model places responsibility for resisting racism in the hands of White European-Americans and provides them with the resources to fulfill this responsibility. Learning about anti-racism from and with one's peers within a safe, educational context, allows for a less defensive, more open response to this sensitive issue. Moreover, offering this structured training to college undergraduate students, a population more prone to self-reflection and personal assessment, provides a vital opportunity for influencing and potentially interrupting the cycle of racism. The pilot group discussed in this paper appears to have facilitated meaningful reflection and change for its members. Replication of this model would provide additional opportunities to assess its value and impact.

Acknowledgements

Special thanks to Javier Cervantes, Jason Chan, Benjamin Harris, Andrea Mondragon, Gaby Ortiz, Shykira Richards and Nichole Smith for their ongoing consultation and expertise during the development of this curriculum. Thanks also to Sharon Chia Claros for linking the group facilitator with the Center for the purposes of this program. Additional thanks to Dianna Stencel for her consultation on the use of mindfulness techniques, Art Munin for his consultation on developing the final session, and Elizabeth Ramirez for her assistance in data analysis. Susan Grossman's feedback and suggestions for drafts are also gratefully acknowledged. The contributions and support from each of these colleagues were invaluable.

References

Akintunde, O. (1999). White racism, White supremacy, White privilege and the social construction of race. *Multicultural Education, 7*(2), 2-8.

Berman-Rossi, T. (1993). The tasks and skills of the social worker across stages of group development. *Social Worker with Groups, 16*(1/2), 69-82.

Bernstein, S. (1973). *Explorations in group work: Essays in theory and practice.* Boston, MA: Milford House.

Dessel, A., Rogge., M., & Garlington, S. (2006). Using intergroup dialogue to promote social justice and change. *Social Work, 51*(4), 303-315.

Drumm, K. (2006). The essential power of group work. *Social Work with Groups, 29*(2/3), 17-31.

Garland, J., Jones, H., & Kolodny, R. (1973). A model for stages of development in social work groups. In S. Bernstein (Ed.), *Explorations in group work: Essays in theory and practice* (pp. 17-71). Boston, MA: Milford House.

Helms, J. E. (1992). *A race is a nice thing to have: A guide to being a White person or understanding the White persons in your life.* Topeka, Kansas: Content Communications.

Kendall, F. E. (2006). *Understanding White privilege: Creating pathways to authentic relationships across race.* New York: Routledge.

Magen, R. (2009). Cognitive-Behavioral. In A. Gitterman & R. Salmon (Eds.), *Encyclopedia of Social Work with Groups* (pp. 25-47). New York: Routledge.

Monkman, M. (1991). Outcome objectives in social work practice: person and environment. *Social Work, 36*(3), 253-258.

Okun, T. (n.d.). *From White racist to White anti-racist: A life-long journey* [PDF document]. *Retrieved from* http://www.cwsworkshop.org/pdfs/CARC/White_Identity/4_Life_Long_ Journey.PDF

Tatum, B. D. (1997). *"Why are all the Black kids sitting together in the cafeteria?": and other conversations about race.* New York: Basic Books.

Tochluk, S. (2008). *Witnessing Whiteness: First steps toward an antiracist practice and culture.* Lanham, Maryland: Rowman & Littlefield Education.

Toseland, R. W., & Rivas, R. F. (2012). *An introduction to group work practice* (6th ed.). Needham, Massachusetts: Allyn & Bacon/Pearson.

Van Dernoot Lipsky, L. (2009). *Trauma stewardship: An everyday guide to caring for self while caring for others.* San Francisco, CA: Berrett-Koehler.

Wise, T. (2010). *Colorblind: The rise of post-racial politics and the retreat from racial equity.* San Francisco, CA: City Lights Books.

Yalom, I. D. (2005). *The theory and practice of group psychotherapy* (5th ed.). New York: Basic Books.

8

De Wallonie et du Québec :

réflexions sur les stratégies de formation visant à développer une culture de l'intervention de groupe chez les étudiants en travail social[1]

Ginette Berteau et Louise Warin

Summary

This chapter addresses the results of a joint study of students registered in courses on social work with groups at a Canadian school of social work (Montreal, Quebec) and a Walloon university college (Liège, Belgium) in fall 2010 and 2011. The authors discuss the role of the facilitators and the obstacles to the development of a group work culture among social work students. As the editors of this volume, we are pleased to respond to the request of the authors that this chapter be presented in French.

Introduction

Cet article présente les résultats et les perspectives suite à une recherche menée conjointement dans une École de travail social québécoise (Montréal, Canada) et dans une Haute École wallonne (Liège, Belgique) auprès d'étudiants inscrits dans un cours sur le travail social auprès des groupes durant les automnes 2010 et 2011. Le but de cette étude s'inscrit dans une réflexion globale sur les possibilités de développer une culture d'intervention de groupe chez les étudiants de baccalauréat en travail social. Une première étape de cette réflexion a été de mener un sondage et des groupes de discussion auprès d'étudiants ayant suivi le cours de travail social de groupe durant les automnes 2010 et 2011. L'article est divisé en sections. La première fait état du contexte de la problématique et des contextes d'enseignement spécifiques. La seconde partie présente sommairement le modèle d'aide mutuelle, modèle de référence commune pour l'enseignement du travail social auprès des groupes. La troisième présente la méthodologie utilisée alors que la quatrième expose les résultats. Dans la cinquième section, le lecteur trouvera l'analyse de ces résultats. Le tout se termine par une réflexion à deux voix qui permet de tirer des conclusions générales et surtout des pistes de réflexion sur les enjeux entourant le développement d'une culture de travail social de groupe chez les étudiants de baccalauréat.

Contexte d'émergence de la problématique

Dans un contexte social d'incertitude et de crise, que ce soit en Europe ou en Amérique, l'intervention sociale de groupe présente plusieurs potentialités pour contrer l'isolement social et développer des réseaux de solidarité et de proximité. Malgré la reconnaissance du groupe comme mode d'aide sur les plans personnel et social, les pratiques d'intervention sociale auprès des groupes restent des initiatives isolées. Partout à travers le monde, la formation à l'intervention de groupe reçoit peu d'attention (Berteau et Warin 2011; Lindsay, Roy, Turcotte et Labarre, 2010; Birnbaum et Wayne, 2000; Knight, 2000). Les recherches mettent aussi en évidence que les intervenants se disent insuffisamment formés avec comme résultat que les pratiques de groupe s'apparentent davantage à des interventions de travail social individuel à l'intérieur de groupe et/ou à des pratiques d'animations ponctuelles. Les processus à l'œuvre au sein du groupe sont peu exploités comme potentiel de changement pour ses membres.

Dans le cadre de symposiums internationaux, deux enseignantes francophones (Liège, Belgique et Montréal, Québec) en travail social de groupe ont partagé ce constat : d'entrée de jeu, les étudiants ne s'inscrivent pas en travail social avec l'intention de développer une pratique de groupe. Ces enseignantes observent, dans le cadre de cours sur le travail social de groupe, que les étudiants arrivent avec une représentation limitée et des présomptions parfois négatives de ce mode d'intervention. Elles constatent aussi qu'une pédagogie appropriée fait diminuer leurs craintes par rapport à cette pratique et que leur intérêt grandit au fil de l'apprentissage. Toutefois, le nombre insuffisant de superviseurs formés et à l'aise dans cette pratique a pour conséquences de limiter les offres de stage dans l'expérimentation de ce mode d'intervention (Knight 2000). La formation pratique étant un élément central dans la construction de l'identité professionnelle, les étudiants ne développent pas suffisamment la culture de cette pratique pour en faire un incontournable dans leurs futures interventions.

Fortes de ces constats, ces enseignantes ont décidé de se saisir de ces enjeux en menant dans le cadre de leur cours respectifs, une recherche conjointe sur la perception des étudiants des deux écoles au sujet de leurs représentations initiales, du développement de leurs connaissances et de leurs habiletés suite au cours sur le travail social de groupe et sur leurs intentions de réaliser un stage en travail social de groupe.

Avant de décrire la méthodologie utilisée, arrêtons-nous sur les caractéristiques de chacun des établissements d'enseignement.

Pour la Haute École Libre Mosane située à Liège en Belgique (HELMo), la formation initiale des assistants sociaux de type non universitaire s'étend sur 3 ans. Elle comprend notamment 385 heures de cours sur les méthodologies de l'intervention sociale et 720 heures de stage et séminaire d'analyse des pratiques. En Bac 1, le cours d'Introduction à la dynamique de groupe de 30 heures se poursuit en Bac 2, par le cours de travail social auprès des groupes obligatoire et qui compte 30 heures. En Bac 3, les étudiants ont la chance de suivre un cours de travail social de groupe optionnel de 20 heures.

À l'École de travail social de l'Université du Québec à Montréal (UQAM), la formation initiale est de niveau universitaire s'étend aussi sur 3 ans. Elle comprend 270 heures de cours sur les méthodologies d'intervention sociale, 750 heures de formation pratique : bénévolat, stage et séminaire d'analyse des pratiques. En début de deuxième année, le cours de travail social auprès des groupes est obligatoire et est d'une durée de 45 heures.

L'enseignement du travail social auprès des groupes

Que cela soit en Belgique ou au Québec, le modèle privilégié pour former les étudiants au travail social auprès des groupes est le modèle d'aide mutuelle de Steinberg (Steinberg, 2004; Steinberg & Lindsay, 2008). Ce modèle vise l'instauration d'une dynamique d'aide mutuelle en amenant les participants à être dans une position aidé-aidant et à devenir des ressources les uns pour les autres. Il place les participants d'un groupe dans une position d'acteurs les incitant à agir sur leur environnement personnel et social. L'intervenant est considéré comme un facilitateur, ce qui le conduit à partager son pouvoir.

Dans le cadre des cours donnés en travail social auprès des groupes dans les deux sites, les étudiants sont d'abord initiés aux fondements de l'aide mutuelle. En cohérence avec le modèle, les étudiants sont aussi instruits à l'importance du processus d'intervention (phase prégroupe, début, travail et fin) ainsi qu'à l'utilisation des processus à l'œuvre dans le groupe comme conditions facilitantes à l'émergence des dynamiques d'aide mutuelle. Pour favoriser l'apprentissage, une pédagogie active dans laquelle les étudiants sont appelés à expérimenter partiellement ou entièrement les phases du processus d'intervention dans une perspective d'aide mutuelle.

Dans le cadre du cours obligatoire en Bac 2 à l'ESAS, les étudiants sont appelés à planifier un projet d'intervention sur base de populations réelles. Toutefois, 30 heures de cours ne suffisent pas à le mettre en application. Dès lors, certains étudiants proposent ces projets aux référents de stage. Le cours donné à l'UQAM étant d'une durée plus longue (45 heures) permet aux étudiants d'expérimenter, depuis 10 ans, l'ensemble du processus d'intervention par l'expérimentation d'un projet d'intervention de groupe axé sur l'aide mutuelle de quatre rencontres avec des personnes nouvellement arrivées au Québec.

Sondage et groupes de discussion

Méthodologie utilisée (2010-2012)

Désirant poursuivre une réflexion commune sur l'évolution des apprentissages réalisés dans ces deux cours de travail social auprès des groupes axés sur l'aide mutuelle ainsi que sur l'évolution de l'intérêt à l'égard de ce type d'intervention, les deux professeures ont décidé d'entreprendre une recherche non subventionnée. Entre décembre 2010 et mai 2012, trois sondages ont été administrés et quatre groupes de discussion ont été organisés auprès des étudiants ayant fréquenté le cours obligatoire de travail social de groupe à Liège et à Montréal. Cette méthodologie à la fois quantitative et qualitative s'étant modifiée au cours du processus, nous présentons celle-ci chronologiquement.

Les sondages

Sur le plan quantitatif, un questionnaire de type sondage a été conçu en décembre 2010. Ce sondage a été structuré en cinq sections. Les trois premières avaient pour but de cerner les représentations du travail social de l'étudiant avant son entrée dans les programmes de formation, l'évolution de celles-ci ainsi que les éléments déclencheurs de ce changement. La quatrième section a porté sur ces représentations de la spécificité du travail social auprès des groupes ainsi que sur les apprentissages faits dans le cours. La cinquième section a été consacrée à identifier les habiletés acquises et qui restent encore à développer après le cours. Cette section a été construite à partir d'un répertoire d'habiletés (Berteau, 2006) qui comprend quatre catégories d'habiletés soient : les habiletés permettant de stimuler les interactions, d'encourager la responsabilité du groupe à l'égard de son processus de groupe, de développer le système d'aide mutuelle et de stimuler la réalisation de la cible commune.

Le questionnaire était de type fermé, avec choix multiples. Quelques questions ouvertes ont été posées en vue de recueillir des commentaires. Les étudiants étaient libres de participer à ce sondage. Ils ont signé à cet effet un formulaire de consentement.

À l'automne 2010, le sondage a été complété en fin de cours, tandis qu'en 2011-2012, après un enrichissement de la section sur les habiletés (phases prégroupe et de début), il a été administré en début et fin de cours. À l'ESAS, 62,5 % de la cohorte des étudiants, soient 195 étudiants, âgés en moyenne de 20,2 ans y ont participé. Du côté de l'UQAM, 25 % des étudiants pour un total de 71 étudiants, âgés en moyenne de 27,5 ans ont complété les trois sondages. Dans les deux sites, la très grande majorité des participants étaient des jeunes femmes (80 % et plus).

Les groupes de discussion

Quatre groupes de discussion eurent lieu. Les trois premiers ont eu lieu au printemps 2011 et avaient pour but d'approfondir les résultats du sondage de 2010. L'échantillon sélectionné de manière aléatoire était constitué d'étudiants ayant répondu au sondage. Chaque groupe devait accueillir au minimum un garçon. Deux de ces groupes eurent lieu à l'ESAS (6 et 7 étudiants) et un à l'UQAM (5 étudiants).

Au printemps 2012, un groupe de discussion a été réalisé à l'ESAS auprès de 5 étudiants de 3e année de baccalauréat pratiquant une intervention de groupe en stage. Il avait comme objectif de récolter les opinions des étudiants sur la qualité du cursus de formation à l'intervention sociale de groupe et plus particulièrement sur le nouveau cours optionnel proposé depuis septembre 2011 en Bac 3.

Résultats des sondages

Les résultats sont traités à partir de la compilation des données chiffrées des sondages et des commentaires libres exprimés lors des sondages.

Les représentations du travail social

Une première question interpellait les étudiants au sujet de leurs représentations du travail social. Cette question voulait vérifier si les étudiants inscrivaient dans leurs représentations, le travail social auprès des groupes. Les résultats du sondage de 2011 (avant le cours) ont clairement laissé entrevoir que cette perspective était déjà présente chez les étudiants des deux sites. La comparaison avec les résultats du sondage après (2011) indiquait suite au cours, une augmentation de 10 % de répondants insérant une perspective de travail social de groupe dans leur perception du travail social.

Cependant, des différences de résultat entre les deux cohortes étaient relevées. À l'ESAS, sur deux ans, 21,5 % des répondants ont eu tendance à situer davantage le travail social comme étant un travail avec les individus et les groupes alors que 56,7 % de deux cohortes de l'UQAM ont positionné le travail social auprès des groupes dans une perspective intégrée, c'est-à-dire qu'ils considéraient que le travail social est à la fois du travail social avec les individus, les groupes et la collectivité. Remarquons aussi qu'au point de départ, que pour plus de la moitié des étudiants, tout site confondu, percevaient que le travail social de groupe utilise les mêmes techniques que l'intervention individuelle.

Les résultats ont aussi mis en évidence, pour les étudiants des deux sites, les mêmes éléments déclencheurs du changement de représentation du travail social. Ces éléments déclencheurs étaient par ordre d'importance : les cours (en particulier les cours de méthodologie de l'intervention), l'exposition à la pratique (stage d'observation, bénévolat, rencontres de professionnels et d'enseignants, l'expérimentation), l'échange avec les pairs (rencontres, discussions et travaux de groupe entre étudiants) et les lectures.

Perception des apprentissages réalisés

Nous avons aussi demandé aux étudiants quels étaient les apprentissages majeurs réalisés dans les cours respectifs. Voici sous forme de tableau la perception des apprentissages que les répondants ont considéré avoir faits :

De façon générale, les répondants de l'UQAM ont semblé avoir retiré davantage d'apprentissages que ceux de l'ESAS, l'écart étant plus important en ce qui concerne la préparation de l'intervention et l'utilisation du modèle d'aide mutuelle.

Une question qualitative portait sur le principal apprentissage fait dans ce cours. Pour les deux sites, l'apprentissage le plus annoté se rapportait à la découverte de la richesse de l'aide mutuelle et à

Tableau I
Perceptions des apprentissages réalisés

Perceptions des apprentissages	UQAM (Montréal) 2010 2011	ESAS (Liège) 2010 2011
Comprendre les fondements de l'aide mutuelle	87,5 % 90	85 % 77,5
Préparer une intervention de groupe	90 % 90	77,5 % 77,5
Utiliser le modèle de l'aide mutuelle	80 % 87,5	70 % 67,5

l'importance des quatre phases d'intervention. Pour les étudiants de l'ESAS, les commentaires furent plus nombreux concernant l'apprentissage de la phase prégroupe et pour l'UQAM, ceux sur l'apprentissage de la phase de travail ont occupé une place prépondérante. Cet écart dans les résultats peut s'expliquer par les différences de contexte d'enseignement.

Perception du développement d'habiletés

Lors du sondage de 2011, nous avons aussi demandé aux étudiants leur perception sur l'importance qu'ils accordaient aux habiletés de la phase prégroupe et de début. Cette récolte de données s'est faite à l'aide d'une question ouverte. De façon spontanée, les cohortes interrogées ont semblé réaliser la complexité de la phase prégroupe et l'importance de préparer minutieusement le groupe. Les répondants ont semblé avoir retenu la nécessité de cerner la problématique et les besoins communs, de définir le but initial, les objectifs et la composition du groupe en fonction de ces besoins communs, de réfléchir à la structuration du groupe et de formaliser le projet d'intervention. Par ailleurs, les étudiants des deux sites ont peu noté l'influence du contexte organisationnel sur les pratiques de groupe.

Par rapport à la phase de début, à l'UQAM tout comme à l'ESAS, les étudiants ont nommé aisément la nécessité lors de cette phase de mettre en oeuvre des habiletés favorisant un climat de confiance, de sécurité afin de mettre en place un cadre propice à la cohésion du groupe et à l'émergence de l'aide mutuelle.

Par contre, malgré l'insistance dans les deux cours sur la clarification du but, des objectifs et des normes du groupe avec le groupe ainsi du rôle de l'intervenant, les répondants des deux sites n'ont pas identifié ces habiletés comme importantes.

Puis, à l'aide du répertoire d'habiletés (Berteau 2006), les étudiants avaient à indiquer leur degré d'aisance face à l'acquisition d'habiletés suite au cours. Du côté de l'UQAM, les habiletés avec lesquelles les étudiants ont semblé à l'aise après le cours (2010-2011) étaient, par ordre de priorité, les suivantes : énoncer et favoriser la création de normes et de règles d'organisation démocratique, inviter les membres à construire sur les idées des autres, favoriser l'interaction entre les membres du groupe et entre le groupe et l'intervenant, encourager la participation collective, favoriser la cohésion, tenir compte de la culture du groupe, rechercher des terrains communs, susciter des points de vue différents, structurer un programme d'activités selon les besoins et établir des buts avec le groupe. Dans les commentaires qualitatifs, plusieurs ont mentionné l'importance de ne pas se positionner comme expert du groupe.

Du côté de l'ESAS, les étudiants semblent avoir identifié la nécessité de développer, par ordre de priorité, ces habiletés : rechercher les éléments communs, encourager la participation collective, énoncer et favoriser la création de normes et de règles d'organisation démocratiques, tenir compte de la culture du groupe, encourager les activités et les actions collectives, renforcer l'importance du travail de groupe, renforcer et souligner les comportements d'aide mutuelle, inviter les membres à construire sur les idées des autres, établir des buts avec le groupe et laisser le groupe agir par lui-même.

Les répondants des deux lieux d'enseignement avaient aussi à repérer les habiletés qu'ils considéraient ne pas avoir suffisamment développées. Pour l'ensemble des cohortes, des habiletés telles que soutenir les efforts d'inclusion et protéger les membres contre de possibles attaques du groupe et être réceptif aux communications voilées et les rendre claire. Notons toutefois que les étudiants de l'UQAM ont nettement identifié après le cours que l'utilisation de stratégies permettant l'expérimentation à l'intérieur et à l'extérieur du groupe leur paraissait particulièrement difficile. Les résultats ont dénoté aussi plus clairement leur malaise en ce qui concerne la gestion de conflit et la recherche de consensus. Par contre, les résultats concernant les habiletés davantage reliées au travail sur le but commun ne sont pas ressortis clairement. À titre d'exemple, à l'UQAM, en 2010 et 2011, seulement 12 % des répondants y ont fait allusion au moment de cocher la progression des apprentissages faits dans les cours.

Les répondants de l'ESAS, quant à eux, appréhendaient dans une future pratique les habiletés suivantes : traduire le processus de groupe au groupe, stimuler l'établissement de normes qui favorisent la contribution des membres et le développement de l'aide mutuelle, généraliser les besoins particuliers dans le but d'établir des terrains communs, savoir saisir le thème commun derrière les messages indirects du groupe, utiliser de façon appropriée la révélation de soi de la part de l'intervenant et à l'intérieur du groupe, appuyer les exigences et les attentes du groupe lorsqu'elles appuient la cible commune du groupe et l'émergence du système d'aide mutuelle, créer un espace sur le plan émotif et physique pour chaque membre, permettre la remise en question de la cible commune et identifier les normes informelles et utiliser des stratégies permettant l'expérimentation à l'intérieur et à l'extérieur du groupe.

Perception des retombées du cours

Les enseignantes ont aussi demandé aux répondants des deux sites s'ils avaient l'intention de faire un stage en travail social de groupe et comment ils envisageaient de réutiliser ce qu'ils avaient appris dans le cours. Le tableau 2 illustre les résultats à ce sujet.

Tableau 2

	UQAM 2010 2011	ESAS 2010 2011
Envisager le transfert du système d'aide mutuelle dans d'autres activités de formation	92 % 90 %	87,5 % 70,10 %
Projeter de faire un stage en travail social de groupe	57,5 % 54, 2 %	57,5 % 33 %
Se sentir prêt à effectuer une intervention de groupe en stage	76,5 % 75 %	57,5 % 65 %

Ce tableau met aussi en évidence que les étudiants de l'UQAM ont semblé davantage prêts à expérimenter l'aide mutuelle dans d'autres contextes tout de suite après le cours. Ces résultats ont peu varié d'une année à l'autre. Par contre, les étudiants de l'ESAS se sont dits moins prêts à expérimenter l'aide mutuelle dans d'autres contextes. Au contraire des étudiants de l'UQAM, un écart important entre les résultats obtenus dans les deux années surtout sur le plan de la projection de faire un stage en intervention de groupe, est observé. Manifestement, les résultats illustraient que même s'ils se sentaient prêts, ils n'avaient pas l'intention de faire un stage en intervention de groupe.

Commentaires sur les résultats des sondages

Les réflexions suivantes sont à partager quant aux résultats des sondages : de façon convergente, le fait que des étudiants en travail social suivent un cours sur le travail social auprès des groupes contribue à ancrer celui-ci dans leurs représentations du travail social. Les étudiants des deux sites considèrent que le cours leur permet de bien comprendre les fondements de l'aide mutuelle, ce qui est au point de départ, un aspect positif. Ils sont aussi d'accord pour reconnaître la complexité de l'intervention de groupe, l'importance et la nécessité de la phase prégroupe et sont en mesure de reconnaître les habiletés clés liées la phase de début.

Par contre, les autres résultats ont démontré constamment un écart dans les perceptions des deux cohortes, et plus particulièrement lorsqu'il s'agit de parler de la progression des apprentissages liée aux habiletés d'intervention. C'est le cas pour les apprentissages concernant la préparation de l'intervention et l'utilisation du modèle mutuelle, pour la perception du développement des habiletés de même que pour l'intention d'utiliser l'aide mutuelle dans d'autres contextes. Cette différence dans les résultats est selon nous attribuable au fait que les étudiants de l'ESAS ne sont pas, en fin de cours en Bac 2, formés à la phase de travail et à la phase de fin d'intervention tandis que ceux de l'UQAM ont la chance d'expérimenter un court projet d'intervention qui les confrontent à l'ensemble des phases. Il est clair aussi que les étudiants du site québécois ont pu commencer à intégrer des habiletés centrales liées à la stimulation des interactions et au développement de l'aide mutuelle. De plus, lorsque ces mêmes étudiants identifient comme habileté difficile, celle d'utiliser de stratégies permettant l'expérimentation à l'intérieur et à l'extérieur du groupe, les enseignantes pensent que ceux-ci commencent aussi à réaliser la complexité des moyens pour atteindre les objectifs du groupe et leur transfert à l'extérieur du groupe.

Il est aussi intéressant de constater que les étudiants des deux sites traitent de la nécessité de définir le but initial du groupe lors de la phase prégroupe, mais reprennent peu la notion du travail avec le groupe sur le but commun lorsqu'ils commentent la phase de début et les habiletés de la phase de travail.

Résultats des groupes de discussion

Pour affiner le sens de ces résultats et pour pouvoir développer une stratégie permettant de consolider la place de l'enseignement du travail social auprès des groupes, nous avons organisé dans chacun des lieux des groupes de discussion à divers moments de la recherche.

Les groupes de discussion suite au sondage de 2010 et qui avait comme but de faire réagir aux résultats du sondage ont confirmé les données recueillies dans le sondage. Les étudiants ont réitéré leur appréciation du cours et leur intérêt pour le travail social auprès des groupes. Le modèle d'aide mutuelle est attractif pour eux. Clairement, l'expérimentation du projet d'intervention à l'UQAM est ressortie comme un élément catalyseur d'apprentissage. Les participants au groupe de discussion de ce site ont noté aussi que la formule a permis à chacun de développer ses habiletés en fonction de son évolution. Par contre, les répondants de l'ESAS ont mentionné comme limite de ne pas pouvoir expérimenter la phase-travail par le biais d'un projet d'intervention.

Tant au Québec qu'en Belgique, les participants à ces deux premiers groupes de discussion se sont dits intéressés à transférer l'aide mutuelle dans différentes situations telles que les travaux en équipe. Selon leur milieu d'appartenance, ils ont perçu que l'aide mutuelle pourrait être utilisée dans d'autres contextes. Ainsi, les étudiants de l'ESAS ont identifié que des cours comme les séminaires d'analyse des pratiques pouvaient être des lieux propices à l'utilisation de l'aide mutuelle. Pour leur part, les étudiants de l'UQAM ont repéré que certains cours avaient des concepts apparentés (ex. intervention avec les familles et leurs proches et interculturalité). Dans les deux sites, tous considéraient que le contenu du cours sur le travail social auprès des groupes pouvait être transféré en stage. Enfin, les étudiants de l'ESAS ont dit regretter la référence prédominante au travail social individuel dans les contenus des cours généraux. Ces répondants ont aussi repéré des interprétations différentes de la notion d'aide mutuelle chez les enseignants.

Un troisième groupe de discussion s'est tenu en 2012, mais uniquement à l'ESAS a rassemblé cinq des étudiants Bac 3 ayant suivi un nouveau cours optionnel sur le travail social auprès des groupes faisant suite au cours obligatoire, cours consacré à la phase de travail et davantage axé sur des mises en situation. Ces étudiants pratiquant tous une intervention de groupe en stage ont confirmé la nécessité de l'expérimentation pour mettre en oeuvre les habiletés liées au processus du groupe et aux conflits et pour approfondir une réflexion sur la position d'intervenant.

Lors de ce groupe de discussion, les étudiants ont mentionné plusieurs types de freins au réinvestissement des notions apprises dans les cours du travail social de groupe. Parmi ceux-ci, la durée du stage limitée à 340 heures et les caractéristiques du lieu de stage sont nettement ressorties : comment mettre en pratique un groupe axé sur l'aide mutuelle lorsque le milieu de stage a une mission d'aide sous contrainte ou comment, en l'absence d'intervention sociale de groupe dans un lieu de stage, intervenir auprès d'un groupe sans modèle professionnel?

Plusieurs étudiants ont manifesté l'intérêt pour inclure des moments d'autoévaluation des apprentissages dans le cadre du cours de groupe de Bac 2. Ce processus renforcerait par le développement de leurs habiletés et de leur confiance en leur capacité d'intervenir en groupe.

Des étudiants de ce groupe de discussion ont observé que l'intervention auprès des groupes n'est pas toujours reconnue à sa juste valeur par l'ensemble des enseignants et que la qualité de la collaboration entre les superviseurs de stage et enseignants pouvait être un élément d'influence sur le développement d'un projet d'intervention de groupe. La discussion a mis en évidence des besoins en formation et d'accompagnement en stage de travail social auprès des groupes différents selon le profil de l'étudiant en terme d'expérience d'animation de groupe et en fonction du niveau d'anxiété ressentie par celui-ci.

Réflexions à deux voix

De ces diverses investigations, nous apprenons que le fait d'être exposé au modèle d'aide mutuelle crée un engouement pour chez les étudiants qu'ils soient d'origine belge ou québécoise. L'expérimentation dans le cadre d'un cours en travail social auprès des groupes fait naitre un début d'aisance face au travail social auprès des groupes contribuant à désirer s'engager dans une pratique de groupe. Les étudiants des deux sites deviennent aussi conscients de la complexité de l'intervention ainsi que du rôle de l'intervenant. Toutefois, comme plusieurs caressent le rêve de faire leur stage en travail social auprès des groupes, cette complexité ne semble pas trop effrayer.

Les groupes de discussion mettent en évidence que les cours sur le travail social auprès des groupes sont appréciés et éveillent les étudiants à la richesse de l'aide mutuelle. Dans les deux sites, les étudiants détectent les incohérences dans les programmes de formation et le peu de place donné au travail social auprès des groupes. Ils souhaiteraient une meilleure articulation entre les contenus de cours ainsi qu'une approche intégrée dans l'enseignement des cours de méthodologie d'intervention. Les étudiants de la Belgique sont aussi conscients de trois obstacles importants pour permettre une réelle expérimentation : la durée du stage ne permet pas toujours de mettre en place un projet d'intervention de groupe, le travail social auprès des groupes est une pratique minoritaire et les superviseurs de stage ne sont pas toujours préparés à les accompagner dans l'expérimentation de ce mode d'intervention.

Ces constats mettent en évidence que les cours et les stages ne suffisent pas à développer les pratiques de groupe et une culture de l'intervention sociale auprès des groupes chez les futurs travailleurs sociaux. Plusieurs freins sont identifiés : d'abord dans le contexte d'enseignement actuel, le travail social auprès des groupes n'est pas suffisamment reconnu, ce qui cause une rareté d'offres de stage ou encore de lieux de stage proposant aux étudiants des opportunités d'expérimenter des interventions de groupe. Cette rareté est surtout évidente quand les pratiques de travail social auprès des groupes restent une pratique minoritaire. Or, nous le constatons à travers les sondages et les groupes de discussion, l'expérimentation est un déclencheur du « goût de faire du groupe ». Enfin, la peur d'une pratique « inconnue » et le sentiment de ne pas disposer de suffisamment de compétences pour la pratiquer ont un impact sur le désir de pratiquer des interventions de groupe et nécessairement freinent le développement d'une culture de travail social de groupe. Ces freins persuadent de la nécessité d'une vision globale et à long terme de la formation au travail social auprès des groupes qui conçoivent des actions à plusieurs niveaux si l'on veut encourager le développement d'une culture de travail social auprès des étudiants, et soutenir des pratiques qui renforcent les liens sociaux.

Stimulées par ces constats, les deux enseignantes ont décidé de poursuivre la recherche. Une nouvelle étape a débuté à l'automne 2012 et a pour but d'approfondir l'analyse des leviers et des freins au développement d'une culture de l'intervention sociale auprès des groupes. Cette recherche-action comprend deux volets : le premier est de mettre en place un dispositif d'aide mutuelle comme modalité pédagogique dans les Séminaires d'analyse des pratiques à Liège et dans des supervisons de groupe offertes aux étudiants réalisant un stage en intervention sociale de groupe à la maîtrise à Montréal. La pertinence de ce dispositif sera évaluée en collaboration avec les enseignants et les étudiants.

Puis, le deuxième volet consiste à élargir l'action menée en offrant dans chacune des deux villes une formation en travail social auprès des groupes en milieu de pratique. Suite à cette formation, les intervenants intéressés seront invités à accompagner des étudiants désireux d'expérimenter le travail social auprès des groupes en stage. Ces intervenants seront alors sensibilisés aux craintes et aux réactions des étudiants à une première exposition à un réel travail de groupe ainsi qu'à la diversité de leurs besoins de formation sur le sujet. Comme aboutissement à ces formations, la mise en place de communautés de pratiques en travail social auprès des groupes sera stimulée.

Ces différentes actions sont un premier pas vers la consolidation de la formation initiale, du renforcement des pratiques existantes, d'une meilleure articulation entre les milieux de formation et les milieux professionnels. Toutes ces stratégies desservent la même fin : celle de développer une culture de travail social auprès des groupes chez les étudiants. Si ces stratégies sont efficaces, le travail social auprès des groupes deviendra une pratique plus vivante et plus répandue. Le travail social auprès des groupes contribuera ainsi de façon plus active à sortir de leur isolement et de leur impuissance, les populations marginalisées.

Enfin, il importe ici de signaler les limites de cette recherche. D'abord, le fait qu'elle se déroule en Belgique et au Québec nécessite de relever plusieurs défis : la distance, le décalage-horaire, la différence de culture et de systèmes scolaires demandent moult ajustements exigeant de la souplesse et un appel la sensibilité interculturelle. La création d'un sondage commun en est un bon exemple puisqu'il a fallu tenir compte de la structure différente des cours et de la façon de concevoir la notion d'habiletés et de compétences. Le petit nombre d'étudiants ayant participé aux groupes de discussion est une seconde limite. Les enseignantes sont conscientes que ces résultats ne peuvent être généralisés. L'absence de financement de cette recherche constitue une troisième limite puisque sur ce plan, les enseignantes doivent assumer l'ensemble de la démarche. Par contre, la richesse des échanges, les ressources spécifiques de chacune, la passion commune et la volonté de faire progresser le travail social auprès des groupes viennent amenuiser ces obstacles. Dans l'ensemble, cette démarche contribue à sortir les enseignantes de leur isolement comme professeures et comme travailleuses sociales de groupe et leur permet d'actualiser leur passion commune : le travail social auprès des groupes.

Note

Culture : ensemble de connaissances acquises qui permettent de développer le sens critique, le goût et le jugement. (Petit Robert, 2003, p. 611)

Bibliographie

BERTEAU, G. (2006). La pratique de l'intervention de groupe : perceptions, stratégies et enjeux. Ste-Foy : PUQ.

BERTEAU, G. ET WARIN, L (2011). *Former à l'intervention sociale auprès des groupes : une responsabilité collective pour contrer la fragilisation des liens sociaux.* 4e congrès de l'AIFRIS, Genève.

BIRNBAUM, M., WAYNE, J. (2000). Groupwork and foundation generalist education. The necessity of curriculum change, *Journal of Social Work Education,* 36 (2), pp. 347-356.

KNIGHT, C. (2000). Critical content on group work for the undergraduate social work curriculum. *Journal of Baccalaureate Social Work,* 5, pp. 93-112

LINDSAY, J., ROY, V., TURCOTTE, D. et LABARRE, M. (2010). Tendances actuelles au sujet de la formation en service social des groupes. *Intervention*. N° 132, pp. 15-24.

STEINBERG, D. M. (2004). *A mutual-aid approach to working with groups: Helping people help one another* (2nd ed.). Binghamton, NY: The Haworth Press.

STEINBERG, D. M., LINDSAY, J. (2008). *Le travail de groupe : Un modèle axé sur l'aide mutuelle pour aider les personnes à s'entraider.* Québec : Presses de l'Université Laval.

WARIN, L. (2010). Intéresser les étudiants au travail social de groupe : récit d'une pratique belge. Intervention, la revue de l'Ordre des travailleurs sociaux et thérapeutes conjugaux et familiaux du Québec, Numéro 133.

9
Group work with KEG cards: Keys to Emotional Growth

W. J. Casstevens, L. Cloninger and E. Avinor

Introduction

KEG ("Keys to Emotional Growth") Cards were developed by Dr. Eleanor Avinor as a therapeutic tool to uncover emotional responses in relational contexts, and to better assist clients with coming to grips with the issues that brought them into psychotherapy. This article introduces the KEG cards for use in group work. The integrative theoretical base for KEG card development is explained, and general procedures for using KEG cards in group work are identified and discussed. Specific examples for their use with groups are also provided. The need for outcome research on this innovative tool is also noted, and ways to move this forward are also suggested.

Background

KEG Cards are a recently developed and innovative therapeutic tool. The cards offer a combination of original art pictures on one side and guiding therapy questions on the other side to facilitate therapy sessions. They are particularly helpful for group work activities and processes. The acronym KEG stands for "keys to emotional growth." The cards were developed to help clients move through denial and resistance, to more quickly reach and address the issues and concerns for which they are in treatment. Many clients seek the help of psychotherapists and clinical social workers to gain insight, rather than to solve a particular problem; they want to find meaning in their lives, experiences, personal histories, and relationships. Winnicott (1958, 1965, 1971) and Bion (1955, 1967) were pioneers in this area. KEG cards relate to the distinctions between self and subject, connecting between the intrapersonal, interpersonal, and inter-subjective, issues and parts of experience. Each card touches on different fundamental issues and the client chooses the focus; the pictures and the questions offer various topics the client can explore. It is important to recognize that clients can relate differently session-to-session (or even within a single session) to the same card, which can evoke different interpretations that touch different core issues at different times, and that this can also occur during a single session in group work. The cards that many clients choose for such work are those with pictures of a woman reclining on the sofa with flowers around her, a woman holding a baby, and families. The family cards open the door to couples therapy and family therapy.

The strength of KEG cards lies in their flexibility. They can be used in therapy with a psychodynamic focus, and with more structured approaches such as cognitive behavioral therapy (CBT; Beck, A., et al., 1979; Beck, J., 2011) or redecision therapy (Goulding & Goulding, 1979). Redecision therapy combines transactional analysis, cognitive behavioral therapy and gestalt therapy modalities within a single clinical model, and KEG cards incorporate aspects of these components. The general procedures for KEG card use, as described below, highlight how smoothly these uses can translate into the group setting. Artwork on the cards provides an opportunity for clients to explore unconscious elements of early experiences, and the impact that these can have on their present relationships and decision-making. KEG cards represent an integrative approach that creatively draws from many theoretical strands of thought.

Dr. Eleanor Avinor, at the University of Haifa in Israel, created and refined the cards during her years of psychotherapeutic work with clients. The pictures on the cards were either selected from other sources or designed specifically for this purpose. Images include paintings, sketches and photographs done by a variety of artists with different styles. The questions on the back of each card are those that Dr. Avinor has found to be most relevant and therapeutical across a broad spectrum of clients, including anxious clients, clients who experienced trauma, and individuals in early stage dementia. As noted previously, the cards were developed to help clients move through denial and resistance, to more quickly address issues and concerns bringing them into treatment. The Israeli prison system has recognized that inmates benefit from this, and the cards are used throughout the Israeli prison system. In addition, the cards are regularly used in Israeli psychiatric settings that include soldiers and veterans exhibiting symptoms related to trauma and/or suicidal ideation. The cards are also used with Alzheimer's patients and appear to slow the cognitive deterioration associated with this disease (e.g. www.youtube.com/watch?v=iz2Ro8-ENWE).

Because of their strong visual impact and the visceral responses KEG cards can elicit, clients can often use them to move directly in and through work that might otherwise have taken weeks or months of talk therapy. In this chapter, we describe ways to incorporate these cards in therapeutic and psycho-educational group work to enhance the group process and group member outcomes. The theoretical underpinnings of KEG cards are presented, followed by the general procedure for KEG card use. Examples of their application to group work are provided and practical aspects of their use with groups are addressed. We conclude by offering suggestions for research into use of this novel therapeutic tool.

Utilization of KEG Cards

Theoretical Underpinnings

The integrative theoretical basis for KEG cards draws from multiple schools of thought to promote their use in different therapeutic modalities for a wide variety of client needs. Avinor explained her thought process in developing KEG cards as follows:

> Before creating the KEG therapy cards, I thought about 'What is the appropriate theoretical framework for my therapy cards?' and came to the conclusion that there are strong links between many of the theories, overlapping and contradictions, and that all are relevant for my cards. Different strokes for different folks – people need and are helped by different theories and techniques at different stages in their development and in their lives. Therapy is change, dynamic and so is life. Therefore

the cards represent different mind-sets and various approaches to therapy. And so, I created questions that are based on many theories and incorporate different ways of looking at and conducting therapy; the therapist makes her choice according to the vulnerability and resilience of the client. (E. Avinor, personal communication, May, 2012.)

The cards work alongside and in conjunction with several therapeutic models and techniques. Each card touches upon theoretical models using the questions that deal with overlapping and often opposing conceptions of subjectivity, identity and interpersonal relationships. Some questions and cards delve into the unconscious, as presented in the work of Anna and Sigmund Freud, Klein, Winnicott, Lacan, Bion, and others. Many questions are based on cognitive behavioral therapy and deal with the here-and-now issues of present functioning, cognitive distortions and behavioral choices, and so forth (Beck, A., Rush, Shaw, & Emery, 1979; Beck, J., 2011). Young and colleagues' schema theory is the basis of many cards and questions, and the client can delve as deeply as s/he wants – or not at all (Young, Klosko, & Weishaar, 2003). Rogerian person-centered psychotherapy is incorporated, and the questions on the cards offer choices in the spirit of Rogers' (1951) humanistic client-centered approach.

The questions on the cards that relate to transference and counter-transference, projection, and detachment, among other ego defenses and processes, are based in Freud's seminal work (e.g., Freud, 1912, 1933). The questions are phrased such that the clients may choose to examine issues related to the core family unit and early attachment, as discussed below. The artwork helps expose the unconscious through association. These effectively link early experience and transference for the client, and can uncover crucial unconscious elements and connections previously absent from treatment. Winnicott, a follower of Freud, developed work in object relations theory. Winnicott's use of the false self and the true self and his conceptualization of the transitional object are incorporated into the cards (Winnicott, 1958, 1965, 1971).

Family systems theory in family therapy is yet another theoretical strand embedded in the cards, and therefore cards show pictures of real families and pictures of doll families (for those who prefer not to project their feelings on real people). These cards have family therapy-related questions on the back. They allude to relationships, and questions on the back touch upon issues of familial stress. While this can lead to a focus on intense events, it does not necessarily have to do so. If it does, the level of stress experienced by family members/clients can be measured by the Subjective Units of Discomfort (SUDS) scale, and rated from 1 to 100 (e.g., Hope, Heimberg, Juster, & Turk, 2000).

Bowlby and Ainsworth's work on attachment theory, alluded to previously, is another theoretical strand within KEG cards. The idea of attachment as a process was articulated most directly by Bowlby (1951, 1958, 1973), when he described an interactive developmental model and the goal-directed partnership between mother-and-infant. The infant uses the mother as a secure base to explore the environment, knowing they can return to seek safety from the mother if they feel threatened. This is expressed and brought to the therapy session via several cards that depict mother figures interacting with small children. Other pictures show the mother displaying indifference toward the child; both the mother and the child are looking away from each other. The balance between exploration via security and proximity-seeking is the goal-corrected partnership that Bowlby emphasized has important and lasting psychological significance. These pictures help the client retrieve such memories and associations. Ainsworth (1978; Stayton & Ainsworth, 1973) further studied this attachment relationship and created a venue in which mother and infant were observed during a series of brief separations and reunions. The child's responses to separations and reunions became a means for describing individual differences in the quality of the attachment relationship. This is reflected in pictures chosen for KEG cards, and the clients relate using stories of separations, partings, and reunions, all of which become a vital part of therapy sessions in which the client chooses one of these cards.

General procedure for KEG card use

The general procedure for KEG card use is summarized in Table 1 (also see www.youtube.com/watch?v=I-gVrqT4hgU). To start, the facilitator asks clients a question, and clients answer by selecting an appropriate card or cards. For example, the facilitator might ask clients to think of a relationship they have, and then choose a card that represents that relationship as it is and as they would like it to be. The clients place the cards on a flat surface, which can be the floor, a desk, or a table. The position(s) of the card(s) is/are important and will usually change as a session progresses. These changes can represent shifts in aspects of clients' feelings and/or the ways clients are dealing with relevant issues. As clients discuss the relationship, cards are often moved from a beginning position of opposition (e.g., a card may be turned face down or on its side, or be placed in the corner of the spread of cards) to a different position, and new cards may be selected to replace or add to card(s) chosen initially.

The KEG cards continue to guide the direction of the session. The facilitator asks questions about the card(s) to explore how clients feel. The facilitator uses the questions on the back of the KEG card (for some images, additional questions are provided on a second, separate card) and can ask the client(s) to read these questions either silently or aloud, and select a question or questions to answer. The facilitator may add other activities to this basic procedure. For example, a "life line" narrative can be constructed by asking clients to arrange cards they select to represent their lives on the floor or a long table. Clients can then "walk" their life lines and narrate their life stories while pointing at relevant cards (Avinor & Silman, 2010).

When using the cards with groups, families, couples, or individuals, it can be helpful to offer clients access to KEG cards of different sizes and multiple copies of a single card. This will involve the use of more than one set of KEG cards, preferably of different sizes. The authors have found that using one set of medium and one set of large cards is optimal with group work, if these are available.

Ways to incorporate KEG Cards into group work

Introductions, group guidelines, and confidentiality always need to be addressed appropriately at the start of the group. For all exercises described below, confidentiality and safety rules/guidelines need to be developed or reviewed, and agreed to by group members at the start of each session. It is the facilitator's responsibility to ensure this is done.

KEG cards as an ice-breaker in group work

In an affirming exercise that can be used as an "ice-breaker" to introduce the cards, the facilitator invites members as they arrive for group to select a card that represents the best decision they have made in their lives, recently. The facilitator then asks group members to share the card they chose with the group and explain why they chose it; members can share as much or as little as feels comfortable. After a member shares, the facilitator asks the member to select one question from the back of the card to answer. Once this is done, the facilitator asks all group members to reflect on how what was shared might apply to them; depending on time constraints, the facilitator may invite members to volunteer their reflections. During this process, the facilitator can emphasize that there are no wrong or right choices or answers. If necessary, the facilitator can also remind participants to avoid giving advice or feedback to group members who have shared.

Self-reflection exercise in group work

A more in-depth and process-oriented group exercise is for the facilitator to ask group members to select three cards: one representing you now, one representing how you would like to be, and one representing how others see you. The cards can be spread on a large table at the side of the group room, or on a table or the floor in the center of the group's circle of chairs or cushions. The facilitator directs participants to lay out their selected cards in the center of the group, on the table or floor, in a way that feels comfortable, and invites volunteers to present their choices to the group, explaining why the cards were chosen and how s/he feels about them. The facilitator then invites group members to comment on what they feel and relate to, and to focus their comments on how whatever was shared applies to them. It may be necessary for the facilitator to remind participants to avoid giving advice or feedback to the person who shared. Once initiated, this can generate a lively interactive process among group members that may lead to the sharing of additional personal revelations and change. The facilitator assists the group to manage its time and can highlight personal revelations that support desired changes. The facilitator's aim is to support the process of self-exploration in a spirit of gentle inquiry. Further, it is critical that the facilitator avoid pressuring a group member into premature revelations or connections and intervene if group members begin to exert such pressure.

Relationship building exercise in group work

KEG cards also offer group members a chance to examine their interpersonal relationships. The facilitator asks them to choose a card that represents a current relationship. The facilitator then has group members choose another card to represent the relationship they would like to have. Members have the opportunity to identify connections and obstacles between their existing and ideal relationship. The facilitator also notes the placement between the two cards; often there is a gap or space that members are invited to discuss. Members share their responses and the feelings, and the facilitator can invite group members to comment on what they relate to in the material shared. It may be necessary to remind group members to focus these comments on their own feelings and how the material applies to them. As with the previous exercise, this can generate a lively interactive process among group members that may lead to the sharing of additional material and changes in choice of cards and/or their placement. The facilitator will need to assist with time management, and may need to moderate interactions between or among members, if the process gets overly animated.

Choosing a safe place in group work

A final example of KEG card use in group work is an exercise involving choosing one card that represents security, safety, peace, and/or relaxation. This is a critical component of any work with trauma. The facilitator invites group members to "choose a card that represents a safe for you" and an age-appropriate discussion of what a "safe place" is can occur at this point. Once group members select their cards, they place them in the middle of a blank sheet of paper (newsprint or 11" x 17" paper are good sizes for this). Crayons or water soluble markers are provided, and group members are asked to expand the borders of their card, drawing around it on the paper however they wish. The facilitator then invites volunteers to talk about how they feel about their card and what they drew. This exercise requires group members to share materials with one another, by asking for crayons/markers of desired colors. The exercise closes with a "round robin" sharing of how group members feel about their safe place, and ways they can use it. It is important for the facilitator to allow enough time for everyone to share during the closing process.

Table 1
General procedure for KEG card use in group work.

Step	Procedure
Card Selection	The facilitator asks a question or gives a directive according to which group members choose a card or cards, for example: "Choose a card that represents the best decision you have ever made."
Card Placement	Group members place the card(s) on a flat surface, which may be a table, desk or floor. The position(s) of the card(s) is important and often changes during the session, as group members move their chosen cards and/or add different cards.
Talking about the card(s)	The facilitator asks questions about the card(s) and how group members feel. The questions are on the back of the picture card or (for some pictures) continue on a separate card. Alternatively, the facilitator may ask group members to read for themselves the questions on the back of the card and choose which question(s) to answer.
Group Discussion	Group process around the cards will depend on group norms. It is helpful for the facilitator to remind group members at the start of group to: (1) avoid judgment/ feedback, and (2) focus comments on ways other members' observations and/or card choices have helped them, e.g., insights gained, connections made, etc.
Other Activities	The facilitator may add other activities to this procedure. For example, a "life line" narrative exercise can be done by: (a) asking group members to select and arrange cards that represent their lives on the floor, and (b) having them "walk" this life line as they narrate their life stories and point to relevant cards.

Discussion and future directions on KEG card use in group work

KEG cards have been recently developed as an integrative therapeutic approach that lends itself to use in groups, and the cards can be purchased online. We have offered a number of suggestions for incorporating the cards into group exercises in various ways and for a variety of purposes. Research on this clinical tool is in its infancy: A clinical trial of KEG card use with Alzheimer's patients is being prepared in the United States, and unpublished Israeli case studies indicate that positive change can occur rapidly for individual therapy clients using KEG cards. Outcome studies on KEG card use in different venues with different populations and different therapeutic modalities, including group work, need to be conducted. If an ethical human subject research study could be approved and conducted within the Israeli prison system, this would provide system-wide data on KEG card outcomes. Meanwhile, single subject design approaches to research with groups, families, and individuals, could begin to construct this missing link. This innovative tool deserves both recognition and a place in the repertoire of all group workers.

References

Ainsworth, M. D. S., Blehar, M. C., Waters, E., & Wall, S. (1978). *Patterns of attachment: A psychological study of the strange situation.* Hillsdale, NJ: Erlbaum.

Avinor, E., & Silman, Y. J. (2010). *Working with KEG cards: Keys to emotional growth.* Haifa, Israel: http://kegcards.net/

Beck, A., Rush, A. J., Shaw, B. F., & Emery, G. (1979). *Cognitive therapy of depression.* New York: Guilford Press.

Beck, J. (2011). *Cognitive behavior therapy: Basics and beyond.* New York: Guilford Press.

Bion, W. R. (1955). Group dynamics: A re-view. In M. Klein, P. Heiman, & R. E. M. Oney-Kyrle (Eds.) *New Direction in Psychoanalysis* (pp. 440-447). London: Maresfield Reprints.

Bion, W. R. (1967). Notes on Memory and Desire. In E.Bott-Spillius (Ed).

Melanie Klein Today (Vol. 2, pp. 17-21). London: Routledge, 1988.

Bowlby, J. (1973). *Attachment and loss: Separation: Anxiety and anger* (Vol. 2). London: Tavistock Institute of Human Relations.

Bowlby, J. (1951). *Maternal care and mental health*. World Health Organization Monograph.

Bowlby, J. (1958). The nature of the child's tie to his mother. *The International Journal of Psychoanalysis, 39*, 350-373.

Freud, S. (1912). *The dynamics of transference*. Standard Edition, Vol. 12, pp. 97-108.

Freud, S. (1933). *New introductory lectures on psycho-analysis*. New York: W. W. Norton.

Goulding, M. M., & Goulding, R. L. (1979). *Changing lives through redecision therapy*. New York: Grove Press.

Hope, D. A., Heimberg, R. G., Juster, I. A., & Turk, C. L. (2000). *Managing social anxiety: A cognitive-behavioral therapy approach client workbook*. New York: Oxford University Press.

Rogers, C. R. (1951). *Client-centered therapy, its current practice, implications, and theory*. Boston: Houghton Mifflin.

Stayton, D. J., & Ainsworth, M. D. S. (1973). Individual differences in infant responses to brief, everyday separations as related to other infant and maternal behaviors. *Developmental Psychology, 9*, 226-235.

Winnicott, D. W. (1971). *Playing and reality*. Middlesex, England: Penguin.

Winnicott, D.W. (1965). *The maturational process and the facilitating environment*. New York: International Universities Press.

Winnicott, D. W. (1958). *Through paediatrics to psycho-analysis*. London: Hogarth.

Young, J. E., Klosko, J. S., & Weishaar, M. E. (2003). *Schema therapy: A practitioner's guide*. New York: Guilford Press

10
Poster presentations at the 2012 IASWG Symposium

P. Matthew Lozano, Jorune Vysniauskyte Rimkiene, Emily Wilk, and Lauren Phillips

Overview

Each year the IASWG symposia include a series of poster presentations given by symposia attendees. Poster presentations are an alternative to the traditional presentation method. Less formal than a paper presentation, poster presentations highlight an authors' work in a brief visual and interactive format. The poster presentations given at the Long Island Symposium represented an array of group work subjects, with the seventeen posters presented representing authors from eight universities across the globe. The subject areas spanned a multitude of themes, including aging, dating violence, wilderness group work, group leadership, and international practice. The editors of this volume decided to recognize the work presented by a few of the authors of the poster presentations at the Long Island IASWG Symposium. This chapter highlights four of the posters, allowing each author to discuss their topic in a brief format in this chapter.

Understanding the Refugee Experience:
Culturally sensitive group work with resettled Burmese male refugees
P. Matthew Lozano, Loyola University, Chicago, United States

Introduction

While illustrating common themes and problems that impact the Burmese culture, this material will illustrate the benefits of therapeutic group intervention in addressing the complex adjustment and psychosocial needs of Burmese refugees.. The experiences of a group of male Burmese refugees are examined as they resettled in a large midwestern city in the United States. The therapeutic group intervention assessed included aspects of Cognitive Behavior Therapy, Object Relations Theory, and the Strength-Based Perspective; it was facilitated through a prominent refugee-resettlement agency.

Background

In 2011, more than 56,000 refugees resettled in the U.S. (U.S. Department of State, 2012), among them asylum seekers from Africa, Iraq, Bhutan, and Burma. Refugees often endure persecution and subsequent trauma stemming from conflict within their home countries. Despite the promise of a new beginning, their resulting feelings of loss and instability are compounded by apprehension over their future (Hilado, 2010, p. 20).

Burma is host to one of the world's longest refugee crises, with more than 500,000 Burmese seeking asylum in neighboring countries (Barron et al, 2007, p. 1). Nearly 17,000 Burmese immigrated to the U.S. in 2011, fleeing from their government's multiple human rights violations, including murder, rape, and torture (U.S. Department of State, 2012).

Challenges

One difficulty this population faces upon arrival in the United States is the task of adjustment, and some clients often overcompensate based on new circumstances. For example, one woman who previously experienced famine reportedly became a food hoarder. The agency's staff speculated that this behavior stemmed from a fear of recurrence in her former living conditions. Language barriers are also common since clinical staff is dependent on interpreters. If an interpreter is not available through their agency's staff or volunteers, one must be sought out through another cultural agency. Ultimately, interpreters are not always available for every dialect. Another barrier exists in conflicting cultural norms. For instance, the National Association of Social Workers (NASW) Code of Ethics states that "social workers should avoid accepting goods or services from clients as payment" (NASW, 2012). If a clinician accepts a gift from a client, it could be interpreted as a violation of this ethic. However, this ethical refusal could then be interpreted as offensive in the client's native culture, thus resulting in damaged rapport between clinician and client.

Limited resources comprise another challenge, especially in regards to medical needs and employment. Single refugees only receive medical benefits for eight months, after which time they may still be incurring expenses. Refugees aged 45 to 65 are also commonly unable to work due to language differences and medical issues. They then become dependent on other family members or the agency itself for financial support (A. Hilado, personal communication, 6/1/12).

Group composition and theoretical approaches

A therapeutic group intervention attempted to address a wide variety of psychosocial issues including: changing familial roles, domestic violence, and anxiety reduction. The group leader facilitated a long-term group consisting of five male Burmese refugees who were accused of domestic violence or who suffered from Post-Traumatic Stress Disorder (PTSD). The participants ranged in age from 24 to 50, and had recently arrived in the U.S. Groups of 2-3 members met with an interpreter and a group leader bi-weekly for 1 to 1-½ hours during a period of four months. Clients were encouraged to consider the meeting area a safe space where they could openly share their past and present circumstances.

Three different theoretical approaches were employed throughout the process. Cognitive-Behavioral Therapy (CBT) guided clients in recognizing counterproductive patterns of thought and behavior – for example, self-blame for the client's family's circumstances in his home country, loss of self-esteem regarding the client's inability to work, and resentment toward the client's female partner for being able to obtain employment. Object Relations Theory encouraged the clients to recall positive memories of their relations in their home country, which promoted self-empowerment and prevented the suppression of traumatic memories. Lastly, a Strengths-Based Perspective was employed in emphasizing the client's capabilities – for example, educating male clients that full-time parenting constitutes admirable employment in the United States; clients were also encouraged to recognize how much strength is required to endure their home country's conditions, travel to a new country, and adjust to a new life on several different levels.

Group goals

Several goals were established to guide the group's therapeutic process. Cognitive distortions stemming from PTSD were challenged, and clients were encouraged to recollect traumatic memories and resolve any untapped feelings. The group leader sought to assist the participants in: recognizing the physical and emotional effects of trauma; identifying triggers and high-risk situations; learning self-reliance; enhancing coping skills; and pinpointing the impact of trauma on self-esteem, the ability to adjust, and perceptions of control. Members were educated about: emotional regulation; recognizing the effects of certain behaviors on others; and reinforcing self-control. Interpersonal skills were visibly enhanced as communication was improved and social relationship deficits were addressed.

Group benefits

Using Irvin Yalom's therapeutic factors as the context, several benefits emerged from this group's process. Universality was demonstrated when the members shared their similar experiences adjusting to a new country. Cohesion emerged as trust and self-disclosure increased. Social connectedness improved as the clients commiserated, which addressed potential isolation and low self-esteem. Instillation of hope was promoted as members witnessed each other gain full-time employment and learn the English language. The group leader imparted information about the United States' cultural norms regarding male gender roles. Members benefited from catharsis, venting about their combined pressures. The group also functioned as a social microcosm, with members describing maladaptive patterns of behavior and achieving self-awareness and transformation (Yalom, 2005, pgs. 1-75).

Implications for social work

There is a critical need for group work in the therapeutic approach to refugee populations. Basic survival needs must first be considered (i.e., housing, food, clothing), but early intervention with Burmese clients can also address issues of trauma through group work. Burmese populations generally thrive in group treatment because the format parallels the community-based relationships that exist within their native culture. Limited time and funds are obstacles to consider in group intervention; in addition, the multiple responsibilities that clients must manage including English classes, full-time jobs, medical appointments, and family commitments make it even more vital for clinicians and clients to use their time efficiently. Addressing trauma and cultural considerations must be a priority when facilitating groups within this specific population. Lastly, the use of interpreters who originate from the same ethnic community is critical, and the role of gender must also be considered when working with this particular population (A. Hilado, personal communication, 6/1/12).

References

Barron, S., Okell, J., Yin, S. M., VanBik, K., Swain, A., Larkin, E.,...Ewers, K. (2007). *Refugees from Burma: Their Backgrounds and Refugee Experiences.* Washington, DC: Center for Applied Linguistics: Washington, DC.

Hilado, A. (2010). Strengths and Challenges: Using Western Theoretical Approaches in Clinical Social Work Practice with Traumatized Refugees. *Praxis,*10 (Fall 2010), 20 – 34.

National Association of Social Workers. (2012). Code of Ethics. Retrieved from: http://www.socialworkers.org/pubs/code/code.asp

U.S. Department of State. (2012). *FY11 Refugee Admissions Statistics.* Retrieved from: http://www.state.gov/j/prm/releases/statistics/184843. htm

Yalom, I. (2005). *The Theory and Practice of Group Psychotherapy,* 5th Edition. New York: Basic Books.

Group Based Parental Skills Training: Parents' View
Jorune Vysniauskyte Rimkiene,
Vytautas Magnus University, Kaunas, Lithuania

Introduction

Research shows that parental influence on children's social, psychological and cognitive development is essential (Sanders, Markie-Dadds, & Turner, 2003; Desforges & Abouchaar, 2003). It also shows a need for parents to have better preparation for raising young children (Sanders & Ralph, 2004). Researchers and practitioners have developed a variety of behaviourally-oriented individual and group-based programs. However, the core question – how to promote positive parenting in individual or group context – still remains. As Lithuania celebrates the first 20 years of the social work profession, this question continues to be of particular relevance. The country lacks professionally-developed, empirically-measured, parenting training programs. In many cases, the training programs are adopted from foreign models and do not consider what theoretical perspectives, themes, and methods are effective in the national context. Research needs to examine which aspects of the training programs are valuable, and which could be further developed and improved. Meanwhile, research on the effectiveness of prevention methods with the families still does not exist in Lithuania. In this paper, the author provides an analysis of the effectiveness of a group-based Positive Parenting Skills Training Program.

Program description

Program characteristics

Positive Parenting Program (Spanjaard, et al. 2010) is based on three Dutch programs: Opvoeden Zo, the Netherlands Jeugd Institute (NJI) and 3xGoei. All are part of PI Research. It was adapted to fit the Lithuanian culture and was part of the project 'Positive Parenting' funded by the Dutch Government. It was a continuation of the project, Establishment of Children's Rights Protection, monitoring mechanisms on the local level in Lithuania, also funded by the Dutch government. The program has been developed for parents who are raising children ages 3 through 12 who experience occasional behavioural problems. The aims of the program are: to promote good relationships between parents and children; to modify behavioural problems; and to prevent serious problems from developing. Six basic parenting skills were taught during the Positive Parenting Skills Training Program: providing attention; giving effective praise; setting limits; saying 'No'; providing correctional instructions; and determining appropriate punishments.

Participants

In the fall of 2011, parents were recruited through an advertisement placed in one of the secondary schools of Kaunas (the second biggest city in the country). The main motivation to participate in the program was an interest in becoming more educated parents. Nine parents (eight mothers and one father) attended six 2-hour sessions. The group meetings were held once a week. An important aspect of the structure was that each meeting included a short tea break, which provided the opportunity for parents to rest and communicate informally.

Format

Icebreakers, role-playing various parenting scenarios, group discussions, feedback, and reflections were utilized. Home assignments for development of new skills were also employed in a group structure.

Data analysis

To reveal parents' views of the parenting skills training program at the end of the program, parents provided anonymous written reflections about strengths and weaknesses of the program. Thematic analyses was used to examine the data. During all the meetings of the program, the researcher who led the group observed the process of group work, analyzing the effectiveness of training methods, as well as the context and main ideas during group discussions. The researcher noted reflections about group work, particularly the process and content.

Results

Quotes

"I have understood that I need to work with myself, but not to tame the child":

The group participants consistently reported a growth of their own consciousness and talents. Reflections included statements such as "[to] my own astonishment I have grown," and "I have found unexpected things in me." During the discussions, particularly about their home tasks, parents talked of their own growth. The participants shared that between meetings they were able to practice their new skills, talk about new knowledge with the partner and the child, and even reconsider their own role as a parent. For example, one group member stated that 'I have understood that I need to work with myself, but not to tame the child'.

"The attitude of others in the group helped to broaden my own outlook":

Participants also shared about the experience of being a group member. Some of them stressed the importance of the comfortable atmosphere as the best component for learning and sharing. One member stated that "the friendly, supportive atmosphere in the group helped [me] gain new knowledge and skills in the field." Another reported "the group members were very open, well-wishing, not trying to prove [their] own truth, but inclined to share, accept, [and] listen to others'.

Since parental training as a preventive method is still a new social service, participants reported different initial emotions (fear, anxiety, etc.). However, the reflections revealed that the experience of the group dynamic was "very comfortable, very pleasant", and members "felt very free in the group"; clearly the group format was successful. Having analyzed the reflections, it became clear that group format helped the parents develop a broader outlook to childrearing, and the "all in the same boat phenomenon" helped members understand that all families struggle with issues. Members agreed that parent-to-parent support is one of most important factors for a mother or a father, as it helps deal with different kinds of social, emotional, and physical issues of parenthood. They reinforce the idea of mutual aid through statements such as "[I understand] that there also are other people who have similar problems, you just must not be afraid to ask for help." After one assignment was completed, parents stressed that sharing the fears they had about their children let them see that their concerns are universal. Parents commonly reported worries that their children "will become bad people", "will neglect parents in their elderly age", and "would [struggle with] any addictions". The practical experience has allowed the participants to perceive how important it is to share their emotions with others; it helps them gain strength and lets them feel understood and supported. The data supports the group work research that group-based parenting programs appear to be acceptable by the participants (Cunningham et al., 1995; Webster-Stratton et al., 1989).

"I appreciate that it was not only sitting and talking"

One of the themes that arose in the participants' reflections focused on the methods of the training program. Practical methods received high praise by the participants, because they helped parents understand the theory better and gain the parental skills: "using role-play was very helpful (when I was a child), it helped me broaden the outlook"; "I appreciate that it was not just sitting and talking"; "sharing own experiences (and valuing of each method reviewed) was serious work and fun, theory and practice." Some of the participants were motivated enough to try new methods, assignments, and even role-plays at home, and they joyfully reported the positive reactions of their family members. The group noticed that after the parents role-played different scenarios, particularly when they were in the child's shoes, they verbalized a better understanding of their children's own emotions and perceptions. The groups were able to balance theoretical knowledge, practical skills training, and discussions. The participants reported the importance of the new experience, and recommended two additional sessions that could provide comprehensive help in parenting issues. Specifically, they requested knowledge on how to raise children's self-esteem, and the effects of new technologies like Twitter, Facebook, and Cell phones.

Tea breaks and group process

The best place to observe group development was the tea breaks. At the beginning the interaction was formal, going mostly in one-way direction from the group leader. Later, the tea breaks became a place and time to share worries about children, to tell jokes, to speak about other important topics. Even how the tea break developed, such as how parents were sitting around the table and how they felt responsibility to bring food to class (it was their personal decision) had meaning. By the third meeting, the participants started bringing homemade food, and the last meeting was a real feast. The attendance of the meetings was high, which can be interpreted as continued interest to the subject.

Conclusion

Following the approach by Sanders & Ralph (2004, p. 363), which states "family intervention programmes should be tailored in such a way as to respect and not undermine the cultural values, aspirations, traditions and needs of different ethnic group", it was decided to examine parents' view of the effectiveness of foreign-designed group-based Positive Parenting Skills Training Program. Reflections were used to look at the new parental skills training program from parents' perspective, while researchers' reflections validated their conclusions. The results of the evaluation coincide with other findings (Lochman, 1990), that parenting training groups is an effective means of assisting parents to raise children. Participation in the Positive Parenting Skills Training Program provided positive outcomes. The participants reported personal development, and it appeared that the friendly, supportive atmosphere in the group helped members obtain new knowledge, while weekly assignments helped members practice the concepts they learned. The participants reported that the experience was valuable and recommended the program be extended. The changes achieved by acquired parental skills should be evaluated by one year follow-up. Further evaluation involving larger numbers in different areas could give more insight into effectiveness of the tool.

References

Desforges C. & Abouchaar A. (2003). *The Impact of Parental Involvement, Parental Support and Family Education on Pupil Achievement and Adjustment: A Literature Review*. Research Report No 433, Queen's Printer.

Lochman, J. E. (1990). Modification of childhood aggression. Hersen, M.

Eisler, R. M. and Miller, P. M. (eds). *Progress in Behavior Modification,* Vol. 25. New York: Academic Press, 47-85.

Sanders M. R., Markie-Dadds C., & Turner, K. M. T. (2003). *Theoretical, Scientific and Clinical Foundations of the Triple P-Positive Parenting Program: A Population Approach to the Promotion of Parenting Competence.* Parenting Research and Practice Monograph No. 1

Sanders, M. R. & Ralph, A. (2004). Towards a Multi-level Model of Parenting Intervention. Hoghughi, M., Long, N. (eds). *Handbook of Parenting. Ttheory and Research for Practice.* London: Sage, 352-368.

Spanjaard, H., Van Assen, K., Kuriene, A., & Blazaite J. (2010). *Projekto "Pozityvi tevyste" medz*iaga. Bendruomeniu kaitos centras: Vilnius.

Tuckman Goes Backpacking:
Training outdoor student leaders in group work theory and practice
Emily Wilk, MSW, University of Dayton, Ohio, United States

Introduction

The transformative power of wilderness trips for undergraduate students is intrinsically linked to the unfolding group process. This material briefly discusses the need for group work theory and practice to be included as a component of outdoor leadership training in order to promote positive group development. Specific group work knowledge and skills recommended for leaders of outdoor educational trips are identified. Special attention is given to designing student leadership trainings in the context of university outdoor programs. Case examples from an outdoor educational program at an urban mid-western university in the U.S. provide insight into how student leaders can apply principles of group work to the field of outdoor experiential education.

Background

Outdoor experiential education can be effective in facilitating the development of groups (Ewert & Haywood, 1991; Hattie, Marsh, Neill & Richards, 1997). In the context of university outdoor programs, wilderness trips allow students to set group goals, learn cooperative responsibilities, and appreciate individual and collective strengths while simultaneously developing a tolerance for adversity and uncertainty in a unique outdoor setting. Through such expeditions, student participants gain a degree of comfort in the group. As a result they become receptive to new conversations, experiences, and friendships, which enable them to connect more deeply to the greater group experience.

Although student leaders of university outdoor programs possess technical outdoor skills, they often lack the theoretical and practical knowledge of group work, which is essential to enhancing group development. Traditionally, outdoor student leaders gain knowledge of applicable outdoor leadership skills from family camping experiences or through formal training at camps, scouting organizations, or nationally recognized outdoor education institutions such as the National Outdoor Leadership School (Paisley, Furman, & Sibthorp, 2008). In light of the legal and moral responsibilities incumbent upon student leaders to keep participants safe and protect the natural environment, possessing technical outdoor skills is a necessary competency for outdoor leaders (Curtis & Williams, 1999; Priest & Gass, 2005; Shooter, Sibthorp, & Paisley, 2009). When facilitating wilderness trips, however, student leaders must apply group work principles to maximize the development of the group. Group work theorist Bruce Tuckman provides an essential framework that outdoor student leaders can use to enhance individual and collective experiences on wilderness expeditions (Toseland & Rivas, 2012). Key group work principles that are applicable to outdoor trips include: use of activity, time and purpose, group cohesion, mutual aid, stages of group development, problem-solving processes, environmental factors, interpersonal and intrapersonal development, and role of the leader (Collins, 2004; Keer & Gass, 1987; McAvoy, Mitten, Stringer, Steckart, & Sproles, 1996). By educating student leaders in the fundamental principles of group work theory and practice, they can more effectively facilitate group experiences in an outdoor setting.

Suggested group work curriculum for outdoor student leaders

Several ways to create an effective group experience on a wilderness expedition include: setting clear expectations with the ability to be adaptive, using a high degree of communication and understanding among group members, initiating effective decision-making strategies, balancing group productivity and meeting individual needs, sharing leadership responsibilities, utilizing different member's abilities and strengths, reviewing processes, and balancing emotional and rational behavior to meet group goals. The author suggests that comprehensive training for outdoor student leaders should include the following components:

- Group structure
  - Recruitment, membership, orientation, and planning
  - Achieving a cooperative group structure
- Stages of group development
  - Tuckman's model of group development
  - Task and relational dimensions of each stage
  - Transference of learning from experience to new settings
- Group decision making
  - Process
  - Strategies
- Cultural Sensitivity
  - Member behavior
  - Communication style
- Group dynamics
  - Communication
  - Interaction patterns
  - Group cohesion
  - Social integration/influence
  - Group culture
  - Conflict
- Leadership
  - Situational leadership style
  - Facilitating group process
  - Group empowerment
  - Power dynamics
  - Co-leadership

Case study: Group work teaching strategies

During the 2011-2012 academic year at an urban mid-western university, the outdoor student leader curriculum included: weekly meetings, a wilderness spring break institute, a ten-day wilderness medicine certification course, and a challenge course training. As students' knowledge and skills progressed, they assumed additional responsibilities in planning and leading different experiences such as weekend and week-long backpacking trips, challenge course experiences, and on-campus workshops. Educating students in the principles of group work can be achieved through the following activities:

- Classroom lessons: At weekly meetings, a topic or research article is discussed.

- "Teach us" sessions: Students educate other students on a particular topic related to group dynamics and issues.
- Case examples: Students are provided vignettes to discuss and analyze as a small group or as a take-home writing assignment.
- Reflections: One-on-one with a staff member or in small groups to share issues and learnings from a recent experience or program they facilitated.
- Teachable moments: Opportunities may occur during an experience where a staff member or instructor may introduce new knowledge that "fits" with what is occurring.
- Informal conversations: Similar to teachable moments, conversations between a student and staff member or between a student and another student provides an opportunity for students to debrief feelings or experiences that are related to group dynamics or interpersonal relationships.

Conclusion

Group work practitioners and outdoor educators continue to seek innovative and engaging methods that will effectively prepare students to lead groups on wilderness trips. Their efforts, however, must be supplemented with empirical studies to determine the most impactful teaching methods and curriculum. This material provides an outline of suggested topics in an effort to spur discussion among scholars and practitioners with respect to outdoor group work education. Preliminary interviews reveal that outdoor student leaders are particularly interested in linking group development theory and practice to outdoor education. Such a link not only can enhance the development of the group, but also will equip students with the tools to more effectively facilitate group experiences on wilderness trips (including managing difficult situations such as confronting similar aged or older peers who are misbehaving). The author seeks to continue documenting group work educational lessons and activities that are informed by scholarship to develop a comprehensive curriculum for university outdoor programs.

References

Collins, L. (2004). The Lost Art of Group Work in Camping. *Social Work with Groups, 26*(4), 21-41.

Curtis, R. & Williams, D. (1999). Training college wilderness leaders for the new millennium. Retrieved November 11, 2011 from: http://www.

princeton.edu/~oa/leaders/train2k.shtml.

Ewert, A., & Heywood, J. (1991). Group development in the natural environment. *Environment and Behavior, 23*(5), 592-615

Hattie, J., Marsh, H. W., Neill, J. T., & Richards, G. E. (1997). Adventure education and Outward Bound: Out-of-class experiences that make a lasting difference. *Review of Educational Research, 67*(1), 43-87.

Keer, P. & Gass, M. (1987). A group development model for adventure education. *Journal of Experiential Education, 10*(3), 39-46.

McAvoy, L.H., Mitten, D.S., Stringer, L.A., Steckart, J.P., & Sproles, K. (1996). Group development and group dynamics in outdoor education. In L. McAvoy (Eds) *Coalition for Education in the Outdoors Research Symposium Proceedings* (3rd, Bradford Wood, Indiana, January 12-14, 1996) (pp. 51-62). Minnesota: The Coalition.

Paisley, K., Furman, N., & Sibthorp, J. (2008). Student learning in outdoor education: A case study from the National Outdoor Leadership School. *Journal of Experiential Education 30*(3), 201-222.

Priest, S. & Gass, M. (2005). Effective leadership in adventure programming (2nd edition). Champaign, IL: Human Kinetics.

Shooter, W., Sibthorp, J., & Paisley, K. (2009). Outdoor leadership skills: A program perspective. *Journal of Experiential Education, 32*(1), 1-13.

Toseland, R. & Rivas, R. (2011). *An introduction to group work practice.* (7th edition). Boston, MA: Allyn & Bacon.

Homicide Survivors: Supporting Victims' Loved Ones Through Groups

Lauren Phillips, Loyola University, Chicago, United States

Introduction

An estimated 9.3% of adults are affected by the homicide of a relative or close friend, thus becoming homicide survivors (Peterson Armour, 2002). These individuals often experience comorbid symptoms of bereavement and trauma, referred to as complicated grief (Stretesky, Shelley, Hogan, & Unnithan, 2010). This material describes a study of a support group designed for victims' families offered by the State's Attorney's Office Victim Witness Program of a large, Midwestern city. It highlights survivors' psychosocial needs, discusses group process and therapeutic factors, and reviews implications for social work practice.

Research shows that 50% of victims' immediate family members experience symptoms of post-traumatic stress disorder (PTSD), such as hyper-arousal, intrusive thoughts related to the homicide, and avoidance of locations, people or events that cause the survivor to recall the homicide (Amick-McMullan, Kilpatrick, & Resnick, 1991). Consequently, an individual may have difficulty mourning their loss or gaining a much-needed sense of closure. Interactions with the criminal justice system can have a particularly profound impact on survivors' processes of healing. Involvement often prolongs family members' grief, as they are immersed in hearings and meetings with lawyers and other legal personnel (Peterson Armour, 2002; Stretesky, et al., 2010). Additionally, the criminal justice system can become a source of re-traumatization if survivors feel overwhelmed, powerless, or unsupported in the aftermath of the homicide (Stretesky, et al., 2010).

Group formation

To support surviving family members, the victim witness program has offered support groups for over 20 years. The author observed the group over a six-month period. Support group meetings were held in courthouse facilities and open to all loved ones of homicide victims. A children's group was offered in tandem with the adult sessions. An experienced art therapist and rotating victim witness staff facilitated the two-hour weekend morning sessions. Attendance varied from as few as five to more than forty members. Participants were primarily Latina and African American women; many were mothers who had lost children or grandchildren to intimate partner violence or gang-related violence. At least one new member attended group almost every month; thus the atmosphere of each session was strongly influenced by what individuals brought to the meeting. However, consistent themes unite participants' needs and processes that reflect such needs transpire during each group.

Psychosocial needs

Members present with an array of psychosocial challenges. They have suddenly become a widow or mother of a murdered child, and are forced to adjust to this unwelcome new role. Many participants also assume unexpected and difficult parental responsibilities; they must now care for the victim's children, who are also reacting to the trauma. Group members frequently express feelings of being stigmatized by their loss. Friends and relatives no longer know how to relate to them, and so they are isolated from crucial support systems. Survivors feel pressure to "get over" it and "move on." Anniversaries represent particularly difficult times. Homicide survivors must also endure the added burden from the criminal case. The drawn out legal system means it can take several years for the case to reach trial, during which time family members face constant upheaval and uncertainty. Additionally, the verdict will not necessarily result in conviction, making it even more difficult to achieve closure.

Group process

Activities are planned in advance of each session; however, most often the flow of the group dictates whether and how these may be used. Art and music therapy-oriented, projects focus on the narratives survivors create, re-tell, and re-enact. These projects have included sharing poems, writing music, and decorating candles to honor the deceased. Members may also bring in their own letters or poetry, which may become the focus of a group session.

In this way, group becomes a place where members connect with one another and process frightening experiences and emotions in safety. Here, they can share feelings that another audience would find unacceptable. Faith was a commonly discussed topic, as participants confront existential issues related to the traumatic loss. Members spoke of widely different experiences—some turn to faith for strength to get through the day, others avoid the church where their loved one was killed, and many express anger at those who describe their loved one's murder as being part of "God's plan." Conflicts in family relationships resulting from the homicide were also frequently discussed.

Yalom's therapeutic factors abounded in group meetings. Group cohesion, altruism, existential factors, direct sharing of information, and catharsis were particularly apparent (Yalom & Leszcz, 2005). Participants drew strength from one another and benefit from mutual aid, the help they offered one another to achieve their individual goals (Toseland & Rivas, 2005). Participants experienced sustained benefits from long-term involvement with support groups, often continuing years after the homicide.

Some members find solace in the helping process, and feel it is a way of honoring the deceased. Long-term participants continue to use the group as a source of support for challenging interpersonal situations stemming from the traumatic loss, as well as a place to share joys and successes. Veteran members fostered group cohesion by welcoming and engaging new members, offering testimonials about the benefits of becoming involved in the group, and reaching out to one another between sessions to offer encouragement. Many members eventually carry what they learn beyond the group and assume leadership roles in the community. They may organize informal networks that reach out to new survivors, lead self-help groups, and advocate for victims' rights legislation and policies.

Implications for Practice and Considerations for Future Groups

Environmental context potentially impacted the composition of the group. Sessions were held in the courthouse facilities of the State's Attorney's Office. For many participants this was a source of familiarity and comfort they associated with receiving support from victim witness staff. However, for individuals who experienced the criminal justice system as disempowering or re-traumatizing, the setting may actually act as a barrier to participation. Although new locations were repeatedly discussed, no changes were made during the author's observation of the group. A more neutral location could allow individuals with more varied criminal justice experiences to access the group.

At times participants raised grievances with the group, such as how space was used at an annual memorial service for homicide victims. When this occurred, a victim witness administrator attended a session solely to listen to members' concerns, thus reinforcing participants' self-advocacy and encouraging an empowering experience.

Conclusion

Support groups can help survivors deal with psychosocial stressors in the aftermath of homicide (Blakley & Mehr, 2008; Miranda, Molina, & MacVane, 2003). For those comfortable accessing a courthouse environment, a prosecutor's office-based group can offer solace, facilitate long-term healing, and empower participants to live their lives in a way that honors their deceased loved ones.

References

Amick-McMullan, A., Kilpatrick, D. G., Resnick, H. S. (1991). Homicide as a risk factor for PTSD among surviving family members. *Behavior Modification, 15*(4), 545-559. doi: 10.1177/01454455910154005

Blakley, T. L. & Mehr, N. (2008). Common ground: The development of a support group for survivors of homicide loss in a rural community. *Social Work with Groups, 31*(3-4), 239-254. doi: 10.1080/01609510801980971

Miranda, A.O., Molina, B., & MacVane, S. L. (2003). Coping with the murder of a loved one: Counseling survivors of murder victims in groups. *Journal for Specialists in Group Work, 28*(1), 48-63. doi: 10.1177/0193392202250078

Peterson Armour, M. (2002). Experiences of covictims of homicide : Implications for research and practice. *Trauma, Violence and Abuse 3*(2),

109-124. doi: 10.1177/15248380020032002

Stretesky, P. B., Shelley, T. O., Hogan, M. J., & Unnithan, N. P. (2010). Sense-making and secondary victimization among unsolved homicide co-victims. *Journal of Criminal Justice, 38,* 880-888. doi:10.1016/j.jcrimjus.2010.06.003

Toseland, R. & Rivas, R. (2005). *An introduction to group work practice* (5th ed.). Boston: Allen & Bacon.

Yalom, I. & Leszcz, M. (2005). *Theory and practice of group psychotherapy* (5th ed.). New York: Basic Book.

11
Roots and wings: Reflections on AASWG

Ellen Sue Mesbur

This chapter provides the content of the Beulah Rothman Plenary presentation given by Dr. Ellen Sue Mesbur at the 2012 IASWG Long Island Symposium. It focuses on reflections and memories of AASWG (recently renamed IASWG), and hopes for the future of the organization. Weaving her own journey with other AASWG members, Ellen Sue Mesbur highlights themes of looking back, lessons learned, and looking forward.

Introduction

It is such an honour for me to be the speaker for this Beulah Rothman Plenary. Beulah was a role model for me. She was one of the first people I met at the 1981 Hartford symposium, and she befriended and mentored me in many ways. She was blunt, smart, honest, and funny. She reminded me of my mother! During the tumultuous times when we were becoming a membership organization, I was complaining to Beulah that the voices of the "younger" participants were not being heard. Beulah looked at me, pointed her finger and said: "Your time will come!" Well, it did.

Without a doubt, AASWG has been one of the greatest influences in my professional and personal life: through the friendships that began serendipitously at various symposia; the committees and activities in which I participated; the symposia I have attended; and the moments of crisis and growth that characterize our organization. To illuminate my own journey, I solicited memories, milestones and reminiscences from my AASWG colleagues. Over thirty people responded, providing me with a rich tapestry of reflections.

Jonas Salk said, "Good parents give their children roots and wings. Roots to know where home is, wings to fly away and exercise what's been taught them" (Retrieved from: http://www.people.ubr.com/education/by-first-name/j/jonas-salk/jonas-salk-quotes.aspx).

AASWG has nurtured the roots of groupwork, and has been a major force in revitalizing practice and education. Bringing educators, practitioners and students together once a year to share knowledge and values, mentoring students and new graduates, and enriching our knowledge through publication and research, has enabled groupwork to take flight.

The memories I received were rich in content, poignant, funny, and abundant with personal life reflections. Four themes emerged from these memories: our history; our milestone events; symposia; and mentorship. Through the words of my colleagues, I will illustrate each of the themes, along with my own observations and analysis.

History and milestones

By understanding our history, we can better understand our present. History teaches us how we made choices. It is a way for us to tell stories and to know what our predecessors did and why. AASWG's history, while relatively short, serves as a way of understanding what compelled a few social work educators to come together to forge a new identity for social groupwork education and practice.

Council on Social Work Education Meeting, 1979

Our organizational history begins in March 1979 at the now famous Council on Social Work Education Annual Program Meeting in Boston, Massachusetts. Ruth Middleman wrote: "...four of us in the hotel lobby looked at the program, aghast at the disappearance of sessions on work with groups. We had come into social work with a background in group work and expected to find more about groups in our national meetings. We put up a little sign by the elevators, 'If You're Interested in Group Work, Come to Room 222 at 6:30 today!'" (Middleman, 1998).

This "groundswell of alarm" was a key event for the formation of the Committee for the Advancement of Social Work with Groups. Lawrence

Shulman recalled: "… Alex Gitterman … and I were attending a CSWE Annual Meeting … when we heard about a meeting for group work teachers … It was chaired by Beulah (Rothman) and Catherine (Papell) …That … evening they proposed the establishment of the CASWG … (we) liked the idea and decided to get involved if we could. Even then we were concerned about the possible threat to group work education posed by the move to generalist practice at such a high level of abstraction you had to look hard to find the practice" (L. Shulman, by email, March 2012).

The first Symposium

Norma Lang, who attended the planning meetings for the first symposium, recalled the sense of purpose and excitement generated by the planners. She noted: "The meeting was characterized by an ambience of great caring, as persons who cared deeply about group work worked to initiate a new era, in which group workers would be able to convene and talk with one another, after a long period with no forum. Beulah (Rothman) and Katy (Papell) had initiated the journal *Social Work with Groups* the previous year (1978), and now we were reaching for a new means to communicate… It was a memorable weekend as we put in place the essential components of that first conference" (N. Lang, by email, April 2012).

The weekend of the first symposium in Cleveland, Ohio in the late fall of 1979 was dramatic and thrilling. Norma Lang described the event: "Everyone who attended that first symposium remembers the 36 inch snowfall on both sides of Lake Erie, making the passage to Cleveland very treacherous, and closing Interstate 90 for several days in the following week. I remember Betty Lewis arranging to house Canadians from the Toronto area until we could travel again" (N. Lang, by email, April 2012).

Urania Glassman remembered many of those first attendees: Paul and Sonny Abels, who chaired the symposium, Ruth Middleman, Katy Papell, Beulah Rothman, William Schwartz, Margaret Hartford, Mary Seguin, Betty Lewis, Anna Fritz, Art Blum, Marge Main, Ruby Pernell, John Ramey, Norma Lang, Harleigh Trecker, Helen Northen, Sylvia Aaron, Gale Goldberg, Al Alissi, Joe Lassner, Sheldon Rose, Harvey Bertcher, Marvin Parnes, Jane Hassinger, Paul Glasser, Charles Garvin, Maeda Galinsky, Ben Zion Shapiro and Norman Goroff. Ronnie also recalls that … "Norma Lang was stuck in the Toronto snowstorm and someone else read her paper; Norma arrived the next day!" (U. Glassman, by email, April 2012).

Alex Gitterman noted: "I vividly recall our giants: Schwartz, Hartford, Lang, etc. – debating current theoretical and practice issues. I do not recall a more intellectually stimulating session. In that conference, I presented my early ideas of integrated practice. The session had a huge turnout and magnificent debate. I recall leaving that conference committing myself to a schizophrenic existence: to developing ideas about integrated practice and, at the same time, to promoting the cause of group work" (A. Gitterman, by email, May 2012).

My own personal recollection of the first symposium was hearing about it from Nell Warren in Toronto, Ontario. We were working together at the YWCA and Nell waxed enthusiastically about her own experience at that conference. I was sorry I had not attended and was determined that I would become involved with the organization.

Becoming a membership organization

The Committee for the Advancement of Social Work with Group was established by Catherine Papell, Beulah Rothman and Ruth Middleman – a formidable triumvirate! Ronnie Glassman, Nancy Sullivan and I remember battles over whether or not we should become a membership organization. In our third year, we did, and became the Association for the Advancement of Social Work with Groups (AASWG). Steve Kraft was brought on board by Katy Papell as our "pro bono" attorney and he "... amended our certificate of incorporation to reflect our name change" (S. Kraft, by email, April 2012).

Chapters

Nancy Sullivan recalled the crisis generated in the association by the formation of chapters. Organizational conflicts related to differing political and philosophical views and issues of "control" characterized those days. Controversies raged in the late 1980's and carried on into the 1990's about what chapters would to do to our organization! "Eventually, Bonnie Englehart, Chapter Development Chair, was successful in entrenching the voice of chapters on the board and on the Executive

Committee. It forced the discussion about recognition of the chapters, diversity and status". (N. Sullivan, Personal communication, March 2012). Steve Kraft remembered "... some of the early tensions as the organization moved to chapter- based, and chapter reps felt that the 'old guard' wasn't always responsive to them" (S. Kraft, by email, April 2012).

National/international directions

Nancy Sullivan noted that "... in the early 1990's, a huge bone of contention was whether AASWG was a national or international association. Although the majority of members were from the United States, there was a strong contingent of Canadians, and growing membership in England, Germany, Ireland and Israel, as well as members from many other countries across the world. For almost a decade, several task forces worked to bring our association to a workable agreement about what we should do and what we would look like as an international association" (N. Sullivan, Personal communication, March 2012).

I became a member of a second iteration of the task force and served as Co-chair, along with the wonderful and wise Ruby Pernell, from 1997-1999. It seems strange now as I recall that it was the US members who paid lip service to the *idea* of being an international organization but struggled with what it would look like in reality. When the Commission on Group Work in Social Work Education was formed, its focus and membership was US-based. At the time, it was crucial for AASWG to have a presence and influence at the Council on Social Work Education (CSWE). The work of AASWG advocates resulted in two important initiatives: a Group Work Stream at CSWE conferences was developed and a partnership established to produce several publications on group work education. Later, I advocated for Canadian inclusion in the Commission and in 2001, I became the first Canadian member of the Commission. I subsequently co-chaired and then chaired the Commission until 2011.

Can we survive?

Nancy Sullivan noted that during her presidential era the big question was "could AASWG be saved?" (N. Sullivan, Personal communication,

March 2012). We were in a crisis of low membership and insufficient funding. We needed to consider the fact that John Ramey, who has been serving as our volunteer General Secretary for many years, along with the wonderful work and support of Carol Ramey, would not be able to continue in that capacity in the future. We had in place a plan for the dignified demise of AASWG. In 1999, Alex Gitterman chaired the *Task Force on Planning for the Future and Restructuring of AASWG*. I was a member of that group and remember the incredible creativity of the sub-groups as we considered various options and opportunities. We survived because of the passion and the labour of love that people gave to the revival and the reconstruction of the organization. Marcia Cohen noted: "Our crisis of a few years ago ... was a distressing time for all of us but I remember how we came together as a powerful and tenacious group and turned things around in terms of membership and finances" (M. Cohen, by email, March 2012).

Michael Wagner remembered ... "It was a real challenge to be on the (AASWG) board through the transition from John and Carol Ramey's "General Secretary" days to what we would become. We imagined being able to function without that level of external support and were so misguided in what we imagined... It was fiercely hard to be part of ... those hard decisions, to accept this vendor or that general secretary or consider this alliance or that exit strategy... It was even hard to see when things began to turn around, when Mike Phillips (AASWG Treasurer) told us we had paid back our debts to the endowment, when our income and our payments matched up again ... that we were through the dark times" (M. Wagner, by email, May 2012).

Tim Kelly recalled: "One of the key moments during my time with AASWG was the transition into the post-John Ramey era. John was central to AASWG and if something happened to him unexpectedly the Association would have been ... in serious jeopardy. John kept asking people to start working towards a post-John Ramey era and for quite a while we kind of put our heads in the sand. Then when we ... realised we needed to start working towards "replacing" John and Carol, John was both relieved and a bit resistant. Yet, he did keep working for a post- JR era...though it was difficult for him and for the Board. One of the key moments was when I was invited to the Ramey's house on behalf of the Executive Committee to get a sense of how AASWG was run from their house in Akron, Ohio. It was like stepping into a museum, as every bit of correspondence and records were all in their house. Over a long weekend John, Carol and I documented all the processes they used, and also began to outline all the records and materials housed at the Ramey's. It was clear that John and Carol were ready to "pass the torch" and we as an organization had to help find a way for that torch to be passed. I was moved by their dedication, commitment and passion to the groupwork cause. .. To see that commitment lived out in their house was humbling. That visit, in a small but important way, helped us as an Executive Committee move forward ... Of course the transition was difficult ... and hit a few snags along the way....but it looks like we made that transition successfully" (T. Kelly, by email, May 2012).

The Standards for Social Work Practice with Groups

Marty Birnbaum noted: "Attention to the Standards has raised the level of group work practice and has given us a sense of pride" (M. Birnbaum, by email, May, 2012). Mary Wilson wrote: "The issue that resonates with me concerns the work undertaken on the Standards. This was such an interesting and stimulating group. Jim Garland was part of this group. He was hugely influential and he was a great mentor to all of us who served then. The continued relevance and application of the Standards is testament to the vision and work of that group. Jim's contribution has been legend...." (M. Wilson, by email, May 2012).

I became involved in two AASWG task forces from 1981 – 1984, where we began looking at Standards for the teaching of social group work in the classroom and in the field. James Garland, Urania Glassman, Charles Garvin and others led the development of those first Standards and left us with a wonderful legacy. For me, as an educator, the Standards have provided us with a rich teaching resource. I crafted an assignment in my group work courses using the Standards as a framework for analysis. In 2009 Carol Cohen and Amy Olshever conducted a survey about the Standards and several symposia have included Think Tanks and discussions led by members of the Practice Committee. Currently, Mark Macgowan is conducting research and writing about students' work with the Standards.

Symposia

The symposia provided the most vivid memories and stories. Traditions and rituals are important elements in the life of an organization. The symposia provide a forum for developing ideas and forming collegial networks, support for "new" presenters, and opportunities for publication through the peer-reviewed proceedings. The following are some of the heart-warming memories from colleagues:

Allan Barsky wrote: "My most memorable moment at an AASWG conference was in Montreal, when we attended a workshop on the use of 'improv' with groups. We must have done 12 different activities, ranging from goofy calisthenics, to freeze-frame improv, to the "let's do [something crazy], and also" game. What a sight to see a group of social work educators acting silly and laughing so hard. I didn't take a single note during the exercises. Still, I remembered the exercises and use them with my classes to this day"(A. Barsky, by email, April 2012).

Andrew Malekoff remembered: "I attended my first AASWG symposium in Toronto in the early 1980's ... Aside from presenting a paper, the spirit and culture of AASWG was contagious. I made a few friends and we had a good time in the city. I was sold. There was very little of the elitist attitude that I had experienced in other academic-oriented settings" (A. Malekoff, by email, March 2012).

Ann Bergart wrote: "Sometime before the 2008 German symposium I became determined to bring the next symposium to Chicago, and we did it! This was also an amazing experience – a huge and ultimately extremely satisfying endeavor. A highlight ... was honoring Katy Papell at Hull House and hearing her letter to Jane Addams ... I attended the Symposium in Cologne, Germany in 2008, though the idea of doing this created a great deal of anxiety. It was a life-changing experience, which included many open and healing conversations. As a result, a burden was finally lifted from my soul -- thanks to the sensitive planning of Ingrun (Masanek) and her committee..." (A. Bergart, by email, March 2012).

Barbara Muskat remembered: "... my first symposium in Quebec (City) - in a session on activities in group work facilitated by Jim Garland, popping balloons with my rear end with some of the 'greats' in group work history! Sitting in another session in Quebec and first meeting you, Ellen Sue. We were listening to Dominique (Steinberg) reading a paper written by someone else who couldn't attend" (B. Muskat, by email, March 2012).

Barbara Jackson wrote: "The 2002 symposium in Brooklyn, New

York was instrumental in getting Commissioner William Bell to allow ACS (Administration for Children's Services) to develop a committee dedicated to strengthening group work In the five years that the committee was operational, they sponsored two group work conferences for ACS and provider agencies. It made it possible for the committee to get ACS to sponsor 40 staff to attend the 2007 symposium in Jersey City The 2008 Symposium in Germany was a fantastic commitment to moving toward an international focus for AASWG For me, every symposium and theme has been special" (B. Jackson, by email, April 2012).

Carol Cohen attended her first symposium in Miami, shortly after Beulah Rothman passed away. She recalls attending a Pre-Symposium Institute facilitated by Jim Garland. Jim was wearing shorts and a T-shirt which, in those days, was quite a statement! She remembers that Jim began with a group work joke, one that she still uses in classes and workshops. Jim asked: "How many of you have been asked to do a group?" After people responded, he asked: "How many of you have been asked to do a client?" This was Jim's wonderful way of reminding us that group workers *lead* and *facilitate* (C. Cohen, Personal communication, March 2012).

Carol Irizzarry remembered: "... My earliest memories of AASWG revolve around the first Toronto symposium in the early 80's I was teaching at Rutgers, one of the Schools of Social Work that had a strong Group Work major... I had been a close friend of Bill Schwartz and his wife Ruth since I studied at Columbia ... It was what we might label now the "Golden Era" of group work, and much excitement was generated among our students who flocked in large numbers to choose this innovative concentration! A month before the Toronto symposium Bill Schwartz died suddenly, which was a devastating blow The symposium committee decided to hold a memorial service for Bill and asked Ruth to attend. She said she would only go if I would speak at the service but I felt quite overwhelmed with grief and didn't think I would be able to get up and talk. Ruth insisted that Bill would have told me I just had to "resolutely make up my mind to pick up the challenge and the courage would follow". As you can imagine I followed this advice and, along with Alex Gitterman and others, I paid tribute to this brilliant teacher and group worker" (C. Irizzarry, by email, May 2012).

Carol Kuechler recalled: "I ... did my first two co-authored presentations at the symposium in Hartford organized by Al Alissi. I met the members of the German chapter of AASWG, which was the beginning of a long time friendship with many members of their chapter over the years since. In Hartford, Hans Erikson and I began the process of organizing our Minnesota members to create a chapter, something we accomplished in one year and, at the 2005 symposium in Minneapolis, celebrated our 10ᵗʰ year as a chapter"(C. Kuechler, by email, May 2012).

Greg Tully remembered: "My first AASWG Symposium was in 2000 in Toronto, and I remember how excited I was to be greeted at the registration table by Norma Lang, and to be welcomed into AASWG by many friendly and esteemed group workers from Canada and around the world. The experience led me to become an active member of the AASWG South Florida Chapter started by Beulah Rothman, with 2001 chapter members that included Toby Berman-Rossi, Tim Kelly, Mark Macgowan, Mark Smith, Laura Farley, Susanne Palombo, and Kathy Sweeney" (G. Tully, by email, April 2012).

Michael Wagner wrote: "Going to Quebec City and experiencing both the internationalism and the collegial tone of the AASWG conference was a great enticement for me. I even submitted a paper for inclusion in the proceedings and was thrilled to have had it accepted... I was one of those 'new practitioner' members of AASWG at the time" (M. Wagner, by email, May 2012).

William Pelech recalled: "... my most enduring memory and the one that has kept me involved with the AASWG was the sense of 'groupness' that I have often felt when coming to the Symposium. The Symposium is qualitatively different than other conferences that I attend. In a way, it feels more like 'coming home for the holidays' than it does an academic conference. This has long been my experience with the AASWG and what keeps me coming back" (W. Pelech, by email, April 2012).

Urania Glassman noted: "Len Kates and I were so fortunate to have the group work association and the symposium because we got to present our theoretical material on group work. Without the feedback and the venue, we never would have been able to write our group work book. This is pretty much how everyone used the AASWG, or CASWG in the earlier years, because we finally had a forum where we could present and generate new ideas, practices, and concepts. We used the symposium to bring it together and energize each other. Many different people did theory building. We held fast to group work's values and practice norms, and to social group work literature as an important base to generate the teaching of group work in the social work programs" (U. Glassman, by email, April 2012).

I attended my first symposium in Hartford, Connecticut in 1981. I was thrilled beyond words to meet Saul Bernstein who appeared rather by email, May 2012).

Marty Birnbaum: "I think the major outlook and struggle has been between the *internal* and *external*. For most of my 25 year tenure on the Board, energy and activity has centered on the internal. Emphasis was on self preservation and organizational maintenance. There was concern that AASWG might not survive. There was reluctance to consider new ideas and taking risks. Various interrelated activities, such as Town Hall meetings, Board retreats, Board composition and leadership and our international focus brought about change in focus and a balance between the internal and external. The results have had a very positive impact and may serve as a model for organizational change" (M. Birnbaum, by email, May 2012). Mary Wilson: "One element that has characterised my association with AASWG is 'Professional Fun'. A group of us have been meeting annually at the Symposium. We have engaged in work together (Global Groupwork Project) but most of all we have had great fun in the doing"! (M. Wilson, by email, May 2012).

Michael Wagner: "I remember each time I had to prepare to say goodbye to those leaders I had started with as they transitioned from the Executive Committee or the Board. Losing Toby (Berman-Rossi) and Roselle (Kurland), watching Tim (Kelly), Ingrun (Masanek), Bob (Salmon) and Mike (Phillips) leave, celebrating their accomplishments and wondering who would step up to take their places. I had to remember that one of the things Bob had taught was that if a group member makes a space, another member will step up into the group role that needs to be played: an idea that takes tremendous courage and exquisite confidence in the power of the group to do its work. And then I watched as you came to that decision, Ellen Sue. I saw in you and in Nancy (Sullivan) in a similar way... the last of us who were there at the beginning when I came on the Executive Committee ... Now we are on the brink of changing our name to try and better reflect an international commitment and reality" (M. Wagner, by email, May 2012).

Urania Glassman: "In the 1980s, the German members started coming (to symposia) and we discovered their strong roots. Also their history, which I think is quite amazing, of having been taught by the group workers who went there (to Germany) after World War II to teach democracy in the small group – Louis Lowy for instance was one of them. Ingrun Masanek is a child of this program, her parents having been in these groups after the war, and Jurgen Kalcher was a young boy after the war and was taught in these groups" (U. Glassman, by email, April 2012).

frail to me until he smiled and spoke – he had the most wonderful eyes and was so welcoming to me. It was there that new friendships were forged; new professional alliances were developed. It was at the symposia where I met the dynamic duo of John and Carol Ramey. They were so welcoming each time we met and their commitment to the AASWG global community was evident in all they did. I was teaching at the School of Social Work at Ryerson University in Toronto and managed to bring Al Alissi, Larry Shulman, Norman Goroff, Judith Lee, and later, Andrew Malekoff, Mary Wilson and Nuala Lordan and Urania Glassman to Ryerson as guest speakers. Imagine how thrilling it was for our students to engage with these wonderful teachers and to be inspired by them. More recently, Urania Glassman, Mark Macgowan, Barbara Muskat, Barbara Neilson, Nancy Sullivan and Patricia Moffat came to my School of Social Work at Renison University College at the University of Waterloo in Waterloo, Ontario. I was a member of the planning committee for the 1982 Toronto symposium and offered my home as a venue for a reception for Board and planning committee members. It was a night to remember! When Toronto hosted the 2000 symposium, I was one of five co-chairs for that Millenium year celebration, along with Deborah Goodman, Norma Lang, Lynne Mitchell, Barbara Muskat, and Nancy Sullivan. Again, our home was open for a reception, and for those baseball fans, watching a key World Series game.

Milestones

In its 34 year history, our association has been through many organizational milestones. What struck me as I was reading the memories sent to me by individuals is that some of us have been affected in profound personal ways through our organizational participation. We have seen the impact of our work on social work with groups through our publications, research, practice and symposia.

Ann Bergart: "A very key AASWG moment for me was meeting Ingrun Masanek. She introduced me when I presented a paper at one of the Symposia. When I heard her German accent I had an intensely visceral response. Most of my parents' families were murdered by the Nazis, and I had been taught to hate and avoid anything or anyone from Germany. I had not done much to challenge this prejudice; the one time I tried led to disastrous results, and I had decided to leave that part of my psyche alone. All this changed when I met Ingrun. She is someone you just have to love – a good, open, joyful human being. I didn't *want* to like her, and that troubled me a great deal. This was the start of what would become a critical personal journey in my life, and I credit AASWG with providing me the opportunity to make that journey"(A. Bergart, by email, March 2012).

Carol Cohen remembers the "professional fun" generated through the symposia and board meetings and the impact of Ingrun Masanek's song: "We are the old people, we are the new people..." (C. Cohen, personal communication, March 2012).

Maeda Galinsky: "AASWG has provided an outlet for social group work. It has brought literature on practice, research and theory to the forefront of the social work community ...The organization has enabled us to see the wide range of group work practice ... Within the group work community, AASWG has encouraged research on group processes and outcomes. In our current emphasis in social work on evidence-based practice it has championed the trend toward increased collection of data so that thoughtful decisions can be made on the basis of data as well as personal experience"(M. Galinsky, by email, April 2012).

Mark Doel: "A key issue for me has been to see the knowledge and thrill that is generated at the symposia reach a wider audience - and the single most significant way to do this is through publication. So, I'm really pleased that AASWG has this strong link with Whiting and Birch through David Whiting, and that the symposium proceedings are quickly coming on stream. Also, as a Member-at-Large on the Board, I've argued passionately for our groupwork knowledge to find publication through peer-reviewed journals so that we can make a splash in other people's ponds as well as our own!" (M. Doel, by email, April 2012).

Joan Letendre: "I served on the Nominations and Elections Committee and co-chaired it with Ellen Sue for several years. This helped me to feel that I was contributing to the future of the organization. I feel that we increased the ethnic, gender and geographical diversity on the board during our tenure. I also feel that we raised consciousness about the importance of reaching out to participants in the conference who might be possible board members in the future and encouraged our committee members as "ambassadors" to be watching out for future leaders. We were rather persistent /ruthless in this way. We also developed the first on-line ballots. Ellen Sue and I had several transnational or international conversations late at night about the kinks in the system and whether we would get enough ballots in, but it always worked out" (J. Letendre,

My own perspective on our organizational milestones is shaped by my participation on the Board, as a member of various committees and task forces, on two symposia planning committees, and attendance at 30 symposia. At the board level, a good deal of our time and energy has focused on our survival as an association, our internal structure and processes, and symposia. I vividly recall those early struggles to become a membership organization, the dynamics amongst the leaders, the debates about the relationship of the chapters to the Board, the tensions around the form of an international association, and the early development and later revisions of the Standards. Despite the internal struggles, each year we have held a symposium, which I believe is the glue that binds us. The symposia generate excitement and new ideas and help us maintain currency and innovation as an organization.

Mentorship

Alan Barsky: "I was presenting on ethical issues in social work at a CSWE conference and an AASWG member suggested that I submit a proposal on ethical issues in social work with groups. (This) turned out to be a very interesting and useful conference, where I could honestly say that the educators were truly practicing what they purported to teach" (A. Barsky, by email, March 2012).

Andrew Malekoff: "I am glad that, over the years, I have been able to return the favor now that I am an 'elder statesman' of sorts. It is great to see my old friends at each symposium and to get to know and to encourage the next generation of group workers and group work scholars and educators"(A. Malekoff, by email, March 2012).

Ann Bergart: "It was serendipity that brought me to AASWG. In applying for an adjunct position teaching group work at Loyola University Chicago, I met Elaine Finnegan, who was very active in the local AASWG Chapter. She asked me to present a workshop at a conference sponsored by the Illinois Chapter. That's how it all started. I met a group of like-minded folks who loved group work. Sometimes you just luck into a group where you know you belong right from the start. That was it for me! ... In the last couple of years I have had the challenge and privilege of co-editing the Proceedings of the 2009 Symposium. This has engaged me in developing new skills, which I am also applying in working with Katy Papell to collect her writings into one volume. Knowing Katy as mentor and friend has been a major highlight of my experience with AASWG" (A. Bergart, by email, March 2012).

Barb Muskat: "My meeting you, Ellen Sue, through AASWG---working together on the Toronto Symposium, working on paper reviews and then how you nurtured my career---teaching at Renison, supporting me to apply for my PhD, and all the really wonderful advice and support you gave me----really changed my career trajectory and cemented my identity as a group worker. Asking Maeda (Galinsky) about how to "manualize" a group---she wrote notes for me on a ripped half sheet of paper that served as the template I used for everything I did on manuals thereafter!" (B. Muskat, by email, March 2012).

Beverley Feigelman: "Alex Gitterman wrote about the use of humor in social work and asked for personal experiences. I sent him some group work vignettes from my work with adolescents in a substance abuse treatment program. Andy Malekoff submitted some vignettes as well and we were published in the next issue. I was very excited to be included with these Group Work greats!" (B. Feigleman, by email, April 2012).

Carol Cohen: Carol attended a symposium session presented by Linda Schiller. It was the first time she had presented her dissertation material on stages of group development through women's perspectives. Carol recalled that Jim Garland was in the room and he was crying. He was so moved and so proud to see his work taken forward and he told Linda: "It's time for new ideas". Carol said that this was such a beautiful loving thing to see and that it has stayed with her throughout the years (C. Cohen, Personal communication, March 2012).

Carol Kuechler: "Katy Papell, John Ramey, Alex Gitterman, Anna Fritz, Alison Johnson and Susan La Lone were my primary mentors. With Jan Andrews, who was also on the board, I learned my way around New York - at least enough to get from our lodging to the meetings" (C. Kuechler, by email, May 2012).

Dominique Moyse Steinberg: "This anecdote comes from my first conference. I was scared to go ... But Roselle (Kurland) assured me that it was a very friendly event, and she was so right. My first morning, I encountered Cy Behroozi, who immediately befriended me. Then, as I stood in line for lunch behind a very tall woman ... turned around, introduced herself, and invited me to sit with her. That was Jan Schopler! I also recall the opening plenary very acutely, because a few amazing things happened: First, I ended up sitting next to Helen Northen, who chatted away with me and, at the end of the evening, told me to 'go get my doctorate'. After that, with Roselle between us as mentee/mentor, we became rather close. On Saturday night at dinner, Roselle leaned over and said to me in a kind of conspiratorial whisper, *'You know that Helen is my mentor. But you know who her mentor was? No,* I replied, *who? Gertrude Wilson. What??* I responded. *Wow!'* And just as I was trying to digest that, she added, *and Grace Coyle was Gertrude's mentor.* At which point I was so awed by my professional lineage that it turned in my head ALL night, leaving me completely sleepless! I am still, today, completely imbued with my lineage!" (D. Steinberg, by email, April 2012).

Donna Mclaughlin: "I recall my very first (AASWG) Board meeting as the Massachusetts Chapter representative. I was a nervous wreck and I didn't know anyone. I was 'star struck' - there sitting across from me were Alex Gitterman and Andy Malekoff, two inspiring writers and group workers. As the day proceeded, I learned how many other well-known group workers were in the room and I was not sure that I could meet the standard, but was sure glad to listen ... It has truly been a privilege to know these mentors (including yourself, Ellen Sue) ... I feel so fortunate. Coming from Boston and being taught by Jim Garland, Lois Levinsky and Trudy Duffy allowed me to learn about AASWG way back when. These are folks who lived group work. I am so glad to have the opportunity to join the neighborhood" (D. Mclaughlin, by email, May 2012).

Flavio Marsiglia: "I was connected to AASWG in the 80s through my dear friend Marjorie Johnson. She invited me to one of the organizing meetings of the NE Ohio Chapter. I felt at home from the start. I was so happy to find other group workers and the rest is history" (F. Marsiglia, by email, March 2012).

Greg Tully: "It was in 2005 that I was asked by my AASWG Chapter Chair to represent the South Florida Chapter at the AASWG Board meetings at the symposium ... When I entered the room I was somewhat nervous and intimidated. I realized that I did not know the 35-40 Board members present, and I prayed no one would ask me to speak because I was convinced I had no worthwhile contribution to make. I must have looked a bit panicked because Mary Lisbon, sitting next to me, leaned over and whispered: 'You look new to all this; don't worry, if you need to know anything I can help you.' This one member's generous outreach was followed by additional welcomes as the weekend progressed, encouraging me to become more dedicated to the AASWG mission...I will never forget how helpful it was to me that one member, Mary Lisbon, extended her support to me. Each day as an AASWG member I try to remember to be as welcoming to any new AASWG members I have the pleasure to meet" (G. Tully, by email, April 2012).

Lynne Mitchell: "I began my career as a group worker in 1986, working with adolescents in one of the most marginalized communities in Toronto. Like most beginning group workers, I was flying by the seat of my pants, isolated, untrained and unsupervised I loved the work and was terrified by it at the same time. I reached out, networked and eventually found my way to something with the perfect name for what I craved: The Toronto Region Groupworkers' Network (TRGN). I began attending meetings and programs, and at one of the meetings, Lee Vittetow, president of the TRGN, approached me and asked me if I would sit on the Executive. I was incredibly flattered; flattery trumped reason and I said yes ... One year, at Ellen Sue's suggestion, I filled in at the AASWG Board meeting for the Toronto Chapter representative who was unable to attend ... it was quite an experience, having more to do with internal politics and less to do with groups than my naïveté imagined, but it was so interesting. Soon after that, Ellen Sue and the nominating committee asked if I would run for the Board. To have someone who I respected, such as Ellen Sue, approach me to run for the AASWG Board, had an incalculable impact on my professional and individual growth. I served in several capacities on the Board over the 2 terms I served. As my swan song, what fun Susan Ciardiello and I had as co chairs of the Marketing Committee! The personal connections have played a tremendously important role in my life"(L. Mitchell, by email, May 2012).

Marcia Cohen: "Toby Berman-Rossi introduced me to group work and to AASWG, back in 1987, for which I will be eternally grateful. We wrote an article together and she became my group work mentor" (M. Cohen, by email, March 2012).

Mark Macgowan: "My first contact with group work was when I had Beulah Rothman as my advisor at Barry (University) when I first started around '89 (she passed soon after). She really inspired my dissertation on engagement in group work (my Chair was David Fike). During those days, the local AASWG chapter brought other luminaries in group work to Miami, such as James Garland, Helen Northen and Charles Garvin. I remember David Fike inviting me to dinner on Miami Beach with Charles Garvin, at the time still Chair of the Doctoral Program. As a doctoral student I was so impressed with his scholarship and involvement with AASWG. After I graduated I went to North Carolina State University and quickly connected with Maeda Galinsky and Jan Schopler. We struggled to get that chapter going, but had fun and learning in the process, and planted some seeds for later growth. Being involved with AASWG for me has meant an opportunity to encounter and engage with those 'greats' of the profession....Alex Gitterman, Marty Birnbaum, Roselle Kurland & Bob Salmon, Judy Lee, Ruby Pernell and of course Katy Papell. This is not to exclude all the others but for me that opportunity to sit with those people has meant being able to pass on the knowledge gained and experiences gleaned to another generation. Thus while I heard about the Association while studying at college, it has been my privilege to pass on the message to the next generation of groupworkers through my teaching and research... both of which have been so well supported by my links with AASWG" (M. Macgowan, by email, March 2012).

Michael Wagner: "It was serendipity that put me in … Bob Salmon's Groupwork course. Bob became a valued mentor and teacher. Bob's experiences and his teaching style and the interplay between Bob's and Roselle Kurland's classrooms created for me a rich well of stories that helped make group clear and focused and useful in my life's work. … In 1999 I was recruited by Ronnie Glassman to help with a conference that AASWG was pulling together with the Educational Alliance and as part of my job there I was to help invite Philip Coltoff to be one of the Keynote Speakers of the day. It was then I discovered that both Phil and Pete Moses, who would be the CEO of CAS after him, were long time AASWG members and I had a convergence of my professional life with my professional association which led to more than a decade of collaborations…Ronnie convinced me to run for Red Apple Chapter Chair, a job I felt totally unprepared to hold, but I ran with the hopes that I could learn quickly" (M. Wagner, by email, May 2012).

Nancy Sullivan: "In 1970's while I was working with CAS as a group worker, Norma Lang was hired as a group work consultant. When the symposium happened in Cleveland in 1979, she recruited me and others to go. Norma encouraged me to go back to school and get a PhD. The first time Norma took me to a board meeting she spent a good deal of time preparing me with tips on how to be "safe" in New York City" (N. Sullivan, Personal communication, March 2012).

Olga Molina: "Roselle Kurland who was a professor of mine during my doctoral studies was the person who encouraged me to join AASWG. Mel Goldstein and Dominique Steinberg were in my doctoral class and they were members who I admired and I decided to join. When I started teaching at Barry University in 2001 I met Toby Berman-Rossi who gave me my first opportunity to teach group work in the graduate program. Greg Tully, Tim Kelly, Mark Smith, and Irene Moreda were all colleagues and active members of the South Florida Chapter. I decided to start going to Symposiums in 2002 and have been going every year since" (O. Molina, by email, March 2012).

Paule McNicoll: "I had been a group worker for 15 years, in many types of settings, before I became a faculty member. When looking for where to disseminate my work, I thought about AASWG. I also had met Larry Shulman briefly when he was teaching at the University of British Columbia. His presence on the Board gave credence to the quality of the organisation and made it appear more accessible. I attended the 1993 Symposium in New York City as a very nervous participant. I was completely awed by the people and the presentations. Roselle Kurland came to talk to me after my presentation and suggested I submit my paper. I owe her an indelible debt for her enthusiasm, her warmth and her guidance. I felt welcome into the midst, by Roselle, but also all other people I encountered. One year I almost stopped breathing when I rode an elevator with the famous Dominique Steinberg; the next year, I was having coffee and chatting with her. Thank you all for being so inclusive. The embrace of other Canadians in attendance was another huge reason why I moved from fear to comfort within the association. At that first meeting in 1993, Alice Home and Esther Blum invited me to share dinners and evenings with them; I attended the conference reception with Jocelyn Lindsay and Margot Breton and they introduced me to all the other Canadians in the room. I remember the feeling of having found a home. The support from Canada never faltered. Ellen Sue Mesbur suggested I run for a position on the Board; Norma Lang, Nancy Sullivan and Lynne Mitchell attended my presentation in Denver and invited me to speak at the Toronto Symposium. My encounters with my Canadian peers reinforced my active commitment to the association" (P. McNicoll, by email, April 2012).

Rochelle Rottenberg: "The first memory I have of AASWG was when I graduated from Hunter in 1981 and was encouraged by Roselle Kurland and Bob Salmon to not only attend the Detroit symposium, but to present on a woman's support group that four other MSW students and I had formed as a result of a class that we all took together. We were very nervous and were well prepared but the only people who showed up for the presentation were Roselle and Bob. However, all four of us ... had a wonderful time at the conference and I have been a member ever since" (R. Rottenberg, by email, March 2012).

Steve Kraft: "My connection to group work began in 1962 as an after-school worker at Lenox Hill Neighborhood Association, but my beginnings with AASWG began with meeting Katy Papell at Adelphi University where I began teaching as an adjunct in 1974. Katy got me involved with the organization in the early 80's as the pro-bono attorney" (S. Kraft, by email, April 2012).

Susan Ciardiello: "I would not be where I am today professionally and academically without AASWG. It all started in 1998 when the assistant director of the agency where I was working gave me the AASWG Call for Papers for the upcoming Symposium in Miami and encouraged me to submit an abstract. She knew Ronnie Glassman and when Ronnie came by the agency she introduced her to me. I was a one-woman group work program at the time-running three children's groups and one adolescent group which I developed on my own initiative. When I met Ronnie she instantly became a mentor and friend. At my first AASWG symposium in Miami, Ronnie introduced me to professors from her university, Marty Birnbaum and Susan Mason, who came to my paper presentation on activities for group work with children. James Garland came to my presentation and told me there was a real need in the field of social group work for a book on activities for group work with children according to the stages of group development. I took his words to heart, and wrote one! Marty Birnbaum, Susan Mason, and Ronnie Glassman, encouraged me to apply to the doctoral program at Wurzweiler School of Social Work. So I did! Ronnie, Marty, and Susan were incredible mentors to me throughout my seven long and sometimes draining years in the doctoral program. They became, along with many other people at AASWG, my group work family. Most of my professional achievements would not have been possible without the encouragement and support I found from the amazing group workers and educators from AASWG. I am currently in the last round of edits for my second book, activities for group work with adolescents. With deep gracious and humble respect, I am dedicating the book to AASWG" (S. Ciardiello, by email, April 2012).

Tim Kelly: "I fell in love with groups during my social work education at the University of Georgia.....yet until I had completed my PhD studies, I had never heard of AASWG. It wasn't until CSWE in Atlanta in 1992 that I finally found out about AASWG. I was walking through the exhibit hall and there was Benj Stempler sitting in a group work booth. I was thrilled to find a group work organization and joined on the spot. I was looking for my first academic job and a professor of mine suggested I meet with the Dean of Barry University while at the conference. I had not heard of the university before and didn't know about the connection to Beulah Rothman. .. I met with the Dean and immediately knew that Barry was the kind of university I wanted. I was invited to interview ... and I was offered a job in what was group work heaven ... The time at Barry seems like my own "Camelot." Of course, while I was there I met my mentor Toby (Berman-Rossi) and I flourished. I was a group worker to the core and a new AASWG member before going to Barry, but I had been an isolated group worker until moving to Barry and being taken under Toby's wing. She opened up so many doors for me and introduced me to so many of my heroes. She also greatly influenced my thinking and helped me develop into the academic that I am today. She also helped me become an active member of AASWG (helped is probably the wrong verb….it assumes one has a choice!). It just goes to show the importance of having committed group workers to bring the next generation along" (T. Kelly, by email, May 2012).

William Pelech: "It started at my first Symposium in Ann Arbor in 1996. When I went to the registration table, I met John and Carol Ramey. I was greeted with a warm smile, handshake and welcome from two lovely people who really cared and were interested in who I was (at that time only a mere doctoral student) and what brought me to the AASWG. I felt that John and Carol were genuinely thrilled to have a new person like me join the AASWG and attend the conference. I have never felt so welcomed in my life at any event... my most enduring memories are the people, from the Ramey's to all of those who attend the Symposium today. This indelible spirit of care, concern, warmth and humanity are what make the AASWG the wonderful organization that it is" (W. Pelech, by email, April 2012).

My mentors: In the early 1980's, I met Lawrence Shulman at a Canadian Association for Social Work Education Conference. I was working on my doctorate and my research focused on the group process in an experiential learning lab. Larry consulted with me and generously mailed me a copy of William Schwartz's doctoral dissertation. In that dissertation Schwartz focused on the role of the educator in teaching and learning and delineated his reciprocal model. When I was struggling with the facilitator's role in those lab groups, Larry reminded me that educational purpose should guide the facilitator, and in the case of the lab groups, the purpose was educational, not therapeutic. This new knowledge shaped my teaching for the rest of my career. An early friendship with Ronnie Glassman, beginning in Hartford, resulted in us writing and presenting numerous papers at AASWG, CSWE conferences. I learned so much from Ronnie and was thrilled when she wrote a second edition of her book so that we could provide our students with her group work wisdom. Jan Schopler and Maeda Galinsky reached out to me in those early years, even offering to house and feed my son James if he was going to study and live in Chapel Hill. Katy Papell,

Alex Gitterman and Dominique Steinberg's works have influenced my teaching and their friendship and support is treasured. Norma Lang, Nancy Sullivan and I have worked together since the first Toronto symposium; Barbara Muskat and Lynne Mitchell have been colleagues since the second Toronto symposium and have provided me with love and support, as well as being great shopping buddies!

Future directions

It is now time to look forward, to build upon our past and create new ways to practice and teach social groupwork. Technology is changing education and practice. It is incumbent upon us to be at the cutting edge of developments in teaching groupwork online, in building networks in person and virtually, embracing creative activities to meet contemporary needs, such as hip-hop, rap and spoken word, developing new ways to connect and build chapters, and to support our colleagues to be involved in shaping educational policies and curriculum. We are faced by global challenges and community tragedies for which we must prepare future practitioners. We have not always "stood our ground" in advocating with our agencies and schools of social work that not everyone can facilitate groups and not everyone can teach social group work. We have specialized theory and training, values and perspectives. We must hold on to this and strengthen that which defines our work.

References

Middleman, R. (1998). *A Brief History of the AASWG by Ruth Middleman,* Social Work with Groups Newsletter, 16(1), p. 17. Retrieved from: http://iaswg.org/Background

Salk, J. Retrieved from: http://www.people.ubr.com/education/by-first-name/j/jonas-salk/jonas-salk-quotes.aspx

Index

Note: the letter "t" after a page number refers to a table.

Lightning Source UK Ltd.
Milton Keynes UK
UKOW03f0725041013

218457UK00002B/24/P